Ecological Healing

Ecological Healing
A Christian Vision

NANCY G. WRIGHT and DONALD KILL

ORBIS BOOKS
Maryknoll, New York 10545

CODEL (the acronym by which Coordination in Development, Inc., is commonly known) is a development aid consortium consisting of 40 Catholic, Protestant, and Orthodox-related groups. These groups have banded together to share their resources for the purpose of encouraging sustainable economic development and the protection of the environment among the poor of the developing nations.

Copyright © 1993 by CODEL (Coordination in Development), Inc.
Published by Orbis Books, Maryknoll, New York 10545 and
CODEL, Inc., 475 Riverside Drive, New York, New York 10115
Manufactured in the United States of America
All rights reserved

Scripture quotations are from the New Revised Standard Version of the Bible copyright © 1989, Division of the Christian Education of the National Council of Churches of Christ in the United States of America, and are used with permission.

Library of Congress Cataloging-in-Publication Data

Wright, Nancy G.
     Ecological healing : a Christian vision / Nancy G. Wright and
Donald Kill.
        p.   cm.
     Includes bibliographical references.
     ISBN 0-88344-932-3 (pbk.)
     1. Human ecology—Religious aspects—Christianity.
     2. Environmental degradation.   I. Kill, Donald.   II. Title.
BT695.5.W75   1993
261.8'36—dc20
                                                        93-25084
                                                          CIP

Contents

Foreword

Since 1969 Coordination in Development, Inc. (CODEL), has given its support to development activities of those peoples who have but scant opportunities to take part in decisions of their economic, social, environmental, and political world. As an ecumenical consortium of about forty Christian development agencies, CODEL supports small-scale, environmentally sound development projects. In support of CODEL's projects, its Environment in Development Program provides education and training to strengthen people's understanding of how to link sustainable management of environmental resources to social and economic well-being. Thus, the Environment in Development Program offers education and training through conferences, workshops, and publications such as the *Guidelines for Planning Series on Environmentally Sound Small-Scale Projects* and the workshop report *Organic Farming in Kenya.* The source of CODEL's concern for environmentally sustainable development is rooted in its Christian commitment to social justice. In this book we offer insights gained in the faith journey we have made with our partners in Africa, Asia, the Pacific, Latin America, the Caribbean, and North America in bringing together care for the Earth and equitable social and economic development. With this publication, CODEL offers its resources, experience, and guidance to all those engaged in similar efforts.

The conclusions of this study flow from the work of many laborers in the vineyard.

In 1989 CODEL began to correspond with fifty members and other friends around the world. These people share CODEL's concern for environment and social development. It was our hope, they knew, to state the case so that Christians concerned with justice and social development issues would turn their attention to environmental concerns critical to the achievement of a just and equitable society. We asked them to send us statements by local churches and from traditional faiths about love for creation; personal testimonies of local people on the topic; books, poems, or articles that address environmental concerns; and case examples of environmentally sound sustainable development based on a faith perspective. The response was heartening. Thirty-six people provided us with a wealth of richly diversified materials, enough to constitute a small library, a moving cry from those concerned, indeed enmeshed, with the plight of the Earth. (We have included some of the material in this volume.) It is our happy responsibility, therefore, to convey our gratitude to all who gave energy, time, and prayerful thought for this enterprise.

The coauthorship gives this account its distinctive perspective. Nancy Wright grew up in the western United States. Her father, a geologist, took the family many times into the mountains and homelands of the Native American peoples, particularly the Navajo. She is a United Church of Christ minister, an editor, and a writer; her graduate studies were in the field of environmental conservation education.

Donald Kill, a Roman Catholic and Columban missionary priest, has spent twelve years as a missionary in the Philippines. Father Kill worked among the poor and oppressed people on the southern Island of Mindanao. It was there, among the indigenous Subanun people, that he was given the gift of understanding more fully the relationship of the human person to nature and the Divine Creator. A native of Toledo, Ohio, Kill brings his third-world experience to this statement of Christian concern.

We would like to express our gratitude for the guidance and support of the members of CODEL's Environment in Development Committee, especially Keith Smiley and John Ostdiek. Other reviewers have also given us invaluable help. Many CODEL members have contributed financial and other types of support. Serge Hughes gave invaluable editorial help. We acknowledge the help and insights provided by Richard Cartwright Austin, particularly on the chapter "The Scriptural View of the Earth and Its Peoples." Finally, we are grateful to the Pew Charitable Trusts for funding the publication of this book in part as a curriculum resource for seminary education training of future church leaders.

CODEL presents this volume in partnership with our members, who are challenged to pursue environmentally sustainable development on a daily basis in Africa, Asia, the Pacific, Latin America, the Caribbean, and North America. They have contributed to the clarity of these reflections. We hope this work will provide support and undergirding for them and other readers as we live and work in these momentous years.

—Rev. Boyd Lowry, Executive Director
—Sr. Mary Ann Smith, M.M., Director,
Environment in Development

INTRODUCTION

Ecological Healing

A Christian Vision

This book is an attempt to plumb the depths of the experience of Christians working in development projects around the world in order to respond from a faith perspective to the environmental crisis so evident in our world today. The book covers many areas. It is important that we achieve some understanding of the historical reasons for ongoing devastation of the environment and the suffering of billions of poor people round the world, despite the aid given by government and private development agencies over the past four decades. The historical perspective includes some economic analysis and summarizes the philosophical and theological presuppositions basic to the prevailing western world-view that bears on the areas of concern.

The U.S. Catholic Bishops have issued a challenge to Christians "to be open to the signs of the times, listen to the word of God, discern together the Spirit's call." What are the signs of our times? We must admit that along with the suffering of the poor they include polluted water and soil, devastated and depleted forests, and an alarming rate of species extinction. What is the word of God? God's word is in a quickened response to biblical texts calling for compassion for the poor and for "justice to roll down like waters." God's word lies in our hearts when we mourn the loss of natural beauty. God's word may be found as we are braced by the writings of Christians, philoso-

1

phers, scientists, and native peoples who are perplexed, as we are, by the stresses and difficulties of the modern world. This book is part of *our* effort to discern the Spirit's call. It is a communal effort, in which we are engaged with people of diverse faiths. Each of us has a partial view, a partial response. Together, as Christ's body, may we live by the Spirit's call, "creating all things new." There is an urgent need for a Christian theology sensitive to our unique living world, our diverse cultures. But can we also develop liturgies to celebrate the beauty and pain of our world, to witness to our connectedness to the natural world and to future generations, and to express the ongoing agony of the struggle for justice? This book will help us reflect, worship, and act in light of the pain and graciousness of the Earth and of human beings.

We live and work in a pluralistic world. Each tradition has its grandeur and its limitations, its successes and failures, and each is attempting to address the question of how the human species should live on Earth. The present environmental crisis calls for a coming together of all people of faith — indigenous peoples from around the world, Catholics, Orthodox, Protestants, Pentecostal and Born-Again Christians, Buddhists and Shintoists, Jews, Moslems, Hindus, and other traditions. In coming together, we people of faith can write a "new story," a story of peace, fellowship, and love of God, one another, and creation.

The benefits of such faith-sharing were exemplified when people of faith convened in Assisi, Italy, in 1986 to witness to their stories, their faith, and their relationship to creation. At this assembly the World Wildlife Federation celebrated its twenty-fifth anniversary by gathering together Buddhists, Hindus, Moslems, Jews, Taoists, Confucianists, and Christians of many denominational traditions, as well as scientists. They blessed the declarations on nature by five of the world's great religions. (Excerpts from four of the statements are provided in Appendix 2 of this volume.) All declarations stated that the beliefs of each tradition will lead believers to conservation.

The coming together of diverse peoples to seek justice and

to renew a commitment to care for this Earth is an encouraging sign for the future. Blessed are we to have such a sign as we discern and witness to the Spirit in this time of danger and awakening.

CHAPTER 1

HEARING THE CRY OF THE POOR

THE NEED FOR CHRISTIANS TO TAKE STOCK

As Christians, have we not been called to help the poor? The prophet Isaiah time and again repeats God's call to show concern for the poor and the oppressed (Isaiah 1:16-17; 10:1-2; 58:6-10). The New Testament records the sermon that Jesus gave in the synagogue, when Jesus quoted from Isaiah and applied the words to himself: "He has sent me to proclaim release to the captives and recovery of sight to the blind, to let the oppressed go free."

This proclamation of Jesus has made the call to bring freedom, joy, and communion to the poor and the oppressed of the world a responsibility of Christians. This special mission to the poor, of necessity, includes response to the plight of species becoming extinct, mineral deposits nearing depletion, dying lakes—and the Earth itself, overburdened with pollution and human population. The calls of Isaiah and Jesus call all Christian people to free the poor and the natural world from oppression, to lift them up for life.

Until very recently many religions, including Christianity, have been slow to respond to the injustice of humans toward the Earth and toward the poor. The relative silence of Christian churches has made them partners in the evolution of the current ecological-justice crisis. The church community, we believe, is called to conversion on this crisis, the ultimate pro-life issue.

5

THE GROWTH OF POVERTY

What are the faces of poverty? What has caused the growth of the number of poor in the last century? An understanding of whom poverty touches and how it does so is necessary in order to change the conditions that create it.

Unjust Land Distribution. Unequal land distribution is a tragic problem in the developing world, particularly in Latin America. This problem partly resulted from colonial invasions and subsequent land appropriations by colonial powers. More recently, large foreign owned and operated corporations acquired huge holdings for growing cash crops (e.g., pineapple, sugar, coffee — most to be sold abroad) and for mining. In Venezuela, 1 percent of land owners own 67 percent of the arable land.

Unjust land distribution creates profound human suffering for millions around the world and promotes environmental destruction. The numbers affected have grown: "Estimated in 1981 at 167 million households . . . the landless and near-landless are expected to increase to nearly 220 million households by the turn of the century."[1] An incredible 92 percent of agricultural families in the Dominican Republic are landless or near-landless. Without land people cannot meet their basic human needs and are vulnerable to malnutrition and ill health. The possibility of employment at adequate wages is often non-existent for the poor. The differences between poor farmers who own their own land and those who do not are illustrated by the following example:

In the Guatemalan village where I lived in the late 1970s, I used to marvel at the elegance with which poor farmers could optimize every available scrap of resources — every ridge of land, every surplus hour of time, every channel of water, every angle of sunlight. Though the Indians where I lived are surely poor, they do own their own plots of land. They depend upon and care for what is theirs. When

I go back to the village, I always find that my friends' fields look just as I remembered them.

Ten years ago, I also worked in Guatemala's northern Quiche province, which, for many reasons, is much poorer than the town where I lived. There, I recall watching in horrified fascination as an Indian farmer and his son planted their plot of corn on a forested slope. The land was so steep that the son had to be held in place with a rope looped around his waist. As he hopped from furrow to furrow, his father let out the slack from around a tree stump.

When I returned to that spot recently, I was not surprised to find that the farmer and his son were no longer there. And neither was the hillside. What remained was a reddish, eroded nub—which looked just like the next and the next and the next former hillside.[2]

The poverty of the environment exacerbates the poverty of the poor in a seemingly endless cycle of degradation. As is apparent in the example above, lack of land forces small farmers to cultivate marginal lands, which quickly erode and are less fertile, leaving another important part of the ecosystem destroyed.

Owning our own land, along with the right to pass it on to future generations, motivates us to care for the land. Indeed, it is not generally known, but true, that the oft-cited economic miracle of Korea was based on governmental redistribution of land.[3] And yet, as we all know, land reform has led to violent clashes and upheaval in countries where privileged sectors resist it.

Population Growth. The last two hundred years have seen an unprecedented growth of human population. In the 1800s we were *one* billion human beings. By 1975 we had increased to *four* billion. At this growth rate, we will be living with *ten* billion people in forty years! "Exponential growth cannot long be sustained without producing stupendous and insupportable numbers of people"[4] given current patterns of food production and consumption, industrial production and distribution, and political and social power.

Africa experiences the greatest population pressure, particularly Kenya, where the growth rate is 4 percent each year — meaning that population will double in just eighteen years. Latin America follows Kenya at 2.3 percent and Asia at 2 percent.

At the present level of low inputs, Africa will be able to support 1,029 million people — a number that will be reached by the year 2005. At this writing, 47 percent of the total African land area is home to more people than it can support.[5]

It is well known that a small population increase in the "developed" world puts far greater pressure on world resources than larger population increases in the "developing" world.[6] Each child born in industrialized societies will consume twenty to forty times as much as a child in the developing world in his or her lifetime — a very unjust distribution of resources.

However, we have seen that poverty and environmental destruction can fuel each other. Many of the world's poor live in tropical areas. There, rain forests and coral reefs, ecosystems that are home to the greatest number and variety of species, are at risk. The poor cut down forests for fuel and clear land and plant in areas that cannot support intensive agriculture. The hungry do not have the time to preserve the soil and forests by rotating crops and implementing fallow periods. In the Philippines and other coastal areas people dynamite fragile coral reefs to stun and capture valuable tropical fish.

High birth rates are symptoms of the failures of a social system, including inadequate family income, malnutrition, poor health care, and minimal or no old age security. High birth rates insure a broader base for family income. If parents bring several children into this world, some usually survive disease and reach adulthood in spite of poor nutrition and minimal health care. Those few who do survive are expected to care for parents in their illness and old age.[7] "This 'strength in numbers' strategy may lower the chances of pulling the whole family out of poverty, but that is a small price to pay if it reduces the risk of falling into starvation."[8]

Other benefits may also come to those who bear large families, including title to more land. In many countries people prize large families as proof of a woman's fertility and a man's virility. Further, greater numbers of children mean a lessening of the burden upon women to find and bring home firewood and water.

Father Sean McDonagh, in *The Greening of the Church*,[9] carefully estimates how a T'boli village of 177 families in the Philippines could continue to use their land in a sustainable manner in the next decades. He believes that they can support their present population increase (4.5 percent annually, a doubling of population in fifteen years) only until the year 2010. He calls for realism in understanding the concept of carrying capacity for humans and other species. Carrying capacity is the number of individuals of any species that an area can support without damage to the web of life in that area. At present we, the human species, appear to be destroying Earth's life-support systems, a clear indication of the urgency of bringing the population back into line with the carrying capacity of the earth.

Poverty and Women. Poor women outnumber poor men. When governments and international bodies gather to discuss the world's problems, women are inadequately represented. Ever since the beginning of the patriarchal age, in which men took over the dominant political and economic role in society, women have had little power. In some societies men hold nearly absolute power. Some cultures have considered the human male as the sole biological creator of human life; by extension, some cultures believe males but not females originate ideas and thus appropriately wield power. Injustice done to women indicates a willingness by men to be unjust to fellow humans. Through this accepted sense of domination men tend to use things — women, natural resources — as they see fit.

In most countries women have had little choice and little voice. It is male-dominated companies and governments that decide that men should be allowed to cut down the forests and destroy the source of the now scarce commodity, fuelwood. Men decide to use pesticides on crops. Yet women most directly suffer the consequences. In societies directly dependent on their immediate environment, girls and women expend increasing energy and time to gather firewood. " 'The boys have nothing to do. For girls it's different. We have to look after the family, collecting firewood as before, but we have to walk further each day to find any' (Sara, an Ethiopian refugee of 14 living in a Somalian camp)."[10] This situation is found the world over. For example, "On the Gujarat plains of India, where fuelwood was traditionally collected once every four days, its depletion means that four to five hours *per day* are now spent collecting in some areas. Up to ten percent of Peruvian women's time is spent in fuelwood collection, while in Gambia, women spend from midday to nightfall every day gathering the evening's supply."[11] The excessive time and energy women spend collecting fuel (and water) means that the family ends up with less food to eat and less time and fuel for its preparation, as well as decreased income. The burden on women becomes crushing.

Deforestation and overpopulation can lead to unwise agricultural practices. As soil deteriorates, women farm for longer hours in backbreaking toil to reap food from poor, hardened ground.

The oppression of women has other practical implications. They receive fewer financial rewards, work more hours, have less education, do more of the household caretaking, and bear and provide for children. "For poor women, as one Brazilian woman says, 'The only holiday . . . is when you are asleep.' "[12] Typically, mothers sleep last and rise first.

When women do work in market economies, their roles tend to be limited to service positions, such as secretarial and clerking ones. Further, women through the centuries have been exploited by various business practices. The early textile industries employed women (and children) as cheap labor in sweat shops. Today in enterprise zones in developing countries around the world women's physical agility and tendencies to compliance make them attractive to employers in assembly-line subsidiary plants of developed-nation companies. The women are employed in flower houses and assembly plants for low pay to perform physically difficult, tedious, and sometimes dangerous work. They are often sexually vulnerable as well. Women have consistently been denied the positions of power needed to alter the directions taken by the societies in which they live.

Youth and Poverty. Children and youth suffer most from lack of potable water and inadequate sanitation. In the Third World only two out of five people have access to safe water and only one in four to proper sanitation. The most serious water-borne disease is diarrhea: "Almost 50% of deaths in the Third World involve children under the age of 5 suffering from some form of this disease . . . Every hour more than 1,000 children die from [it]."[13]

Of the world's absolute poor, two-thirds are below age 15.[14] In their formative years, many millions of children are deprived of sufficient nutrients. Such nutrient deprivation decreases their ability to learn important skills needed to live more productive lives.

Poverty and Labor. Some people who live in more comfortable circumstances look upon the poor as lazy, lacking energy, and undisciplined. And yet, it is the poor who carry the burdens forced upon them by the lifestyle to which the rich have become accustomed.

Generally, when corporations compute the cost of a product the lowest price the labor market will bear is the amount allotted for wages. The result for the working poor is limited and sometimes inhumane working conditions and wages that cannot procure some basic household necessities.

In many countries poor farmers work long hours to produce food that ends up on the tables of the rich, food that the farmer and his family often cannot afford to eat. The Philippines offers stark examples of this phenomenon. In a country where 75 percent of the people are farmers, and where there is an annual shortfall in rice and corn production, the government has allowed transnational corporations to enter the country and to buy up prime agricultural land. Farmers, forced off their land by these corporations, are offered meager compensation. As a further enticement, the farmers are offered jobs on the plantations of the transnational corporations, but at daily wages that are one-third of the hourly wage of workers in the "developed" world. Those plantations produce pineapple and banana crops for export to Japan and other developed nations. The farmers, now laborers, are caught up in a cash economy. When faced with escalating prices of rice and corn, they soon find they cannot afford to eat.

In recent years prime agricultural lands in the Philippines have been converted into brackish ponds in which giant shrimp are grown for export to Japan. Such inappropriate land use takes land away from needed production of rice. But, worse than that, it destroys the soil, making it nearly impossible to return the soil to productive use for growing food for local consumption. All of this occurs so that people in another country can enjoy a delicacy.

THE GAP BETWEEN THE "HAVES" AND THE "HAVE-NOTS"

The gap between the rich and the poor is wide and is, in fact, growing. Although global economic growth has risen moderately, absolute poverty has increased faster than population levels. Adjusted per capita income in India has *decreased* between 1960 and 1990. And "the per capita income of the average Latin American is 9 percent lower today than it was in 1980."[15]

Let us take a look at *all* people living on Earth between 1950 and 1989. In U.S. (1989) dollars adjusted income per person for the rich rose from $3,000 to $12,000; for middle-income people average income rose from $1,000 to $3,400; for the poor average income rose from $500 to $1,500; and for the poorest, income stayed the same, at about $500.

The world's population now totals over five billion people. Sixty percent receives less than $2,000 per capita per year. A smaller group makes between $2,000 to $4,000. Five percent of the world's people live in the top income stratum, most of them in the United States.[16] Absolute poverty—"a condition of life so characterized by malnutrition, illiteracy, disease, high infant mortality and low life expectancy as to be beneath any reasonable definition of human decency"[17] — afflicts 1.2 billion people now, and is expected to afflict 1.5 billion people by 2025.[18] Recent trends in global economics worsen the gap between rich and poor countries. Developed countries erect trade barriers that create strong competition among developing countries trying to sell their commodities. The barriers and competition lower the prices that the developing countries receive for their products. The World Bank and the International Monetary Fund have estimated that economic losses in developing countries due to industrialized nations' trade barriers amount to twice the sum of official development aid.[19]

Massive loans to developing nations by the developed nations in the 1970s and early 1980s led to an economic and environmental disaster. The Third World now owes a staggering 1.2 trillion dollars to richer nations.[20] To pay off this debt, developing countries will have to further deplete their natural resources and jeopardize social programs.

CONCLUSION

How do we stop our progress down the path of widening the gap between the small numbers of wealthier people and much greater numbers of poor people? How can we provide for the needs of humans and avoid depletion of the Earth's resources? A new and just land-use system is needed, one that reflects our respect for other people and for nature's limits and diversity. We need to change institutions and economic priorities to reflect this respect. Many will resist such a reorganizing of life; people who stand to lose financially will exert their power to stop change. Christians, called by Christ to care for the poor and for creation, can be leaders in this movement for structural change.

SUGGESTIONS FOR INDIVIDUAL REFLECTION
OR GROUP DISCUSSION

1. Think about and share with others your answers to these questions:
   a. What are the most obvious situations of poverty in our community? What can we change in order to address the causes of poverty?
   b. What can I (my family, church, organization, community) do to reduce poverty?
   c. How is land owned, divided, and used in our area? Who profits? Who pays?
   d. Are there observable differences in the lives of women and men around us?
   e. Has population grown in our area? If so, what effects has this growth had?

2. What are close-at-hand environmental problems? What are the causes? Who is affected and how? When did the problems start? (For people who are more visual than literal, drawing pictures or charts may be helpful in answering these questions.)

CHAPTER 2

The Environmental Crisis

HUMAN IMPACT ON THE BIOSPHERE

The human species is a late addition in the stunning work of creation. The universe, it is now believed, came into being some fifteen billion years ago. The Earth is young. Only four-and-a-half billion years old. In the mysterious emergence of the Earth, humankind appears to have evolved over a period of roughly 450 thousand years. Thus, humans have lived during one-ten-thousandth of the Earth's life span!

Our knowledge of the universe has moved at a very uneven speed, but clearly the progress of the last three centuries has been phenomenal. In the past one hundred years we have seen deeper into the mysteries of the Earth. The astoundingly complex industrialized economic systems of our day are based on constant growth of markets. This drive, once it assumes systematic form, has achieved wonders. It has also, to our sadness and despair, leveled mountains and plundered resources. The stuff of new mountains is garbage. In order to benefit a minority of humans, the system, the drive, concentrates upon immediate ends, which in the long term precipitates suffering and disintegration.

The consequences of focusing only on immediate ends are frighteningly evident. Humans drain rivers to supply water to far-distant cities and towns and dam valleys in order to store up this water supply. Consumer societies, centered around industrial economies, destroy forests, turning trees into throwaway paper products. Trying to feed growing populations, we developed modern agricultural systems. Grasslands, forests, and wetlands thus give way to plowed fields, which absorb chemical fertilizers. Soil toxicity increases, and after a short period the soil becomes depleted. We pollute the air with acids, the rivers with sewage, the seas with oil. We use high technology to tamper with the atom—the basic building block of all materials—and with the gene, which transmits inheritance for all forms of life.

Some of the cycles of destruction, especially extinction of animal and plant species and global warming, are already beyond the point where we might have avoided extensive damage. Today more and more people are cognizant of this threat, and we make common cause with them.

As Christians we have no choice. We must become stewards of creation. We have been placed on this blessed plot of land to care for it and make it fructify. Creation is a gift.

ENVIRONMENTAL PROBLEMS

Some specific areas of concern are dealt with in a summary fashion below. A detailed discussion of each is far beyond the scope of this volume.

Agricultural Losses. In the United States, one-third of the adults are obese, but one-tenth of the world's people are severely malnourished. "Each year forty million people die from hunger and hunger-related diseases. This figure is the equivalent of more than three hundred Jumbo Jet crashes a day with no survivors, almost half the passengers being children."[1]

Agriculture in many countries around the world is not sustainable either in human or environmental terms. To keep pace with population growth, an additional twenty-eight million tons of grain are required each year. Yet, an estimated fourteen million tons of grain production are lost each year because of environmental degradation.[2] Erosion, desertification, deforestation, and changes in weather patterns take their toll. Thus world food security is falling, not rising, as we ravage the soil. The United Nations estimates that one-third of the agricultural soil available to our world in 1975 may be lost by the end of the century. To form 2.5 cm "of topsoil can take anything from 100 to 2,500 years, depending on the soil type."[3]

In many areas once productive land has become parched and lifeless. This process, particularly acute in Africa, is called *desertification*. It is caused by drought conditions, poor farming methods, and expanding populations. It results in twenty-five million tons of productive topsoil being lost each year. In many areas agricultural procedures have been depleting the soil for centuries. Rich farmlands once stretched across Greece through Asia Minor and Palestine to the Euphrates River. These lands, the bread basket of the Roman Empire, were exhausted and eroded.

The Philippines was once a tropical paradise covered with virgin forests and abundant fruit, grains, and wildlife. On the southern Island of Mindanao the destruction of the forests to provide agricultural land began in the early 1950s with the great influx of farmer settlers from the northern islands after World War Two. At that time farmers could harvest twenty to thirty sacks of corn per acre. Now the yield is only three to five sacks. The once dark rich soils have eroded, leaving barren hillsides, silted rivers, and oft-flooded lowlands.

Modern industrial agriculture can be particularly destructive of the soil. Heavy applications of fertilizers — manufactured from petroleum — produce a greater harvest in the short run. But soil fertility declines, and the soil becomes prone to erosion. Thus ever-increasing quantities of fertilizers are needed to maintain production. Over time, crops produced by these intensive systems lack natural health and resistance and need higher quantities of pesticides. In a vicious cycle, the pesticides pollute the soil, water, and atmosphere and undermine the health of farm workers and consumers. Such a system is not sustainable in the short or long run and has the further disadvantage of decreasing plant diversity.

Modern agriculture reduces the variety of crops cultivated for human use. Although there are an estimated eighty thousand edible plants in the world, humans rely on fewer than twenty varieties for 90 percent of our food.[4] A pest attacking one such crop (for example, maize, wheat, rice, or beans) could bring about widespread starvation in large human populations. Within a generation the majority of industrial farmlands may have limited potential for growing crops. Within that generation petroleum, the base for both synthetic fertilizer and pesticides, is likely to become more scarce and expensive, making the cost of these agricultural additives prohibitive for the average farmer.

The U.S. Committee on Agricultural Sustainability has made very clear the daunting challenges we face in agriculture. The world will need to feed 40 percent more people through sustainable agricultural systems within the next twenty years, despite the fact that we have used almost all the land that can be safely irrigated. Supplies of water in many areas are limited, and many more people are drawing upon them. Over parts of Africa, Asia, and Latin America, the population now exceeds the carrying capacity of local agriculture, and food production per capita has fallen in Africa since 1967, Latin America since 1981, and Asia since 1984. We need heroic *research* efforts to undergird environmentally sound sustainable agriculture, and intensive *practice* of such agriculture, supported by governmental, nongovernmental, and international agencies.

Rain Forest Destruction and Species Loss. Many of us have stood in a forest and felt in its peace the nearness of God. There is a quiet mystery, a sense conveyed by a forest's bird calls, and insect and animal movements, that the Creator's life stirs all around us. Forests are God's creation and are home to millions of creatures, many of whom humans have never even seen or named.

People have always used forest products for fuel, food, shelter, and clothing. Forests are an essential part of the Earth's web of life. Through photosynthesis, they take in carbon dioxide, a gas given off during respiration by animals, including humans. Equally important, they respire, or breathe out, water. Their ability to reprocess water is critical to the world's climate. A tropical rain forest absorbs, stores, and expires water so well that, through natural cycles, it returns to its environment half the rainfall it receives. When tropical forests are cut, regional rainfall becomes erratic. Forests also hold soil, keeping it from running off during rain storms.

Tropical rain forests are especially valuable. They are home to 40 percent of the Earth's species and to half of the Earth's growing wood. Tropical forests once covered nearly 90 percent of the Amazon basin, Guatemala, Panama, Zaire, Sierra Leone, the Ivory Coast, the Philippines, Indonesia, Papua New Guinea, Malaysia, and Thailand.

Today, people cut forty thousand square miles of rain forest each year (equivalent to an acre and a third per second). This threatens not only many of the world's plants and animals but also the way of life of hundreds of groups of indigenous peoples, forest dwellers for millennia. In 1950 the area of the world covered by tropical forest was 15 percent. It is projected to be only 7 percent by the year 2000. At the present rate all the tropical forests will have been felled by the middle of the next century. (By contrast, since 1950 the percentage of land covered by temperate forest has remained constant, around 20 percent. This is due to reforestation.)[5]

Once cleared, tropical forests cannot regenerate themselves as do temperate forests. Except for energy from the sun, nearly all the nourishment for plants and animals within a rain forest circulates through the mostly above-ground ecosystem. These complex forests paradoxically stand on poor soil. When stripped of trees, the soil absorbs the heat of the tropical sun and rises in temperature by as much as ten degrees. These higher temperatures hasten the breakdown of rich organic compounds, which normally nourish plant roots. Forest plants that thrive on these organic chemicals and need the cooler temperature of the forest soil to survive die in the depleted and super-heated soil.

As mentioned, between 40 and 50 percent of the Earth's species live only in the complex environment of stupendous diversity that is the tropical forest. Thomas Berry states:

> The Red Books of threatened and endangered species published by the International Union for Conservation of

Nature and Natural Resources are sobering to look through. The book of vertebrates includes some eight hundred species of higher animals that are presently imperiled in their wilderness habitat. The listing includes some of the most gorgeous expressions of life that have ever been present on the Earth.[6]

Tropical forest cutting is the main cause of species extinctions in the world today. Scientists and others are deeply alarmed; they estimate that between 100 and 300 species become extinct each day — the worst wave of mass extinctions in sixty-five million years.[7] This could possibly mean that one quarter of the Earth's species will become extinct in the next half century.

Extinction of species depletes the gene pool of plants and animals. This gene pool functions somewhat like a gene "bank." Future generations of humans need varieties of plants and animals from which foods and medicines (including possible keys to solving AIDS, cancer, and other health problems) may be developed. A theologian might tell us that when our activities cause the extinction of a species we lose one face of God, one expression of divine beauty, one strand in the web of life connecting us to all else on God's Earth.

Many factors are involved in forest cutting and the extinction of habitat for the African elephant and rhinoceros, along with many other animals and plants. Much of the forest supplies tropical hardwood timber for western European, Japanese, and North American markets. It is not priced according to its value. Yet lifestyles of the privileged minority have emerged in both tropical areas and in the purchasing countries that depend on the marketing of this timber.

Ranchers also clear forests to raise cattle in order to provide cheap beef for fast-food outlets in industrial nations. The once-rich range lands in the industrial countries have been depleted by improper management and over-grazing. Appropriate changes in rangeland management and animal husbandry could lessen pasture degradation and forest cutting.

Poor farmers in the tropics with little or no land holdings

practice the age-old method of "slash and burn" agriculture. This style of farming caused little harm to the forests when the numbers of farmers were few and the forests, as farmers moved on, had many years to regenerate. It is much more destructive now that this is not the case.

Relatively little attention has been given to the economic benefits that derive from harvesting a tropical forest sustainably, that is, without basically altering the forest. Properly managed, a tropical forest can produce nuts, berries, latex, flowers, and many more products of long-term value.

Political concern about tropical forests has grown. Political pressure from constituents can force legislators to remove legal procedures that subsidize the pillage of the forests and instead create laws to protect them.[8]

Animal Husbandry. Herds of wild animals once roamed the world's plains. They lived within natural rhythms. Predator and prey lived out a binding system of checks and balances that protected their habitat.

Human beings first domesticated dogs and then other animals, including cattle, sheep, goats, pigs, geese, and ducks. Humans also killed wild herds for their hides as well as for meat. Such killing at times lapsed into wanton slaughter. One of the most tragic examples is that of the buffalo, which once roamed the plains of the western United States. The European immigrants to North America and their descendants killed buffalo for entertainment and also to bring into submission the Native Americans, who depended on buffalo for food, clothing, and shelter. The expertise of the Native Americans in range management went unrecognized. In Africa the slaughter of African elephants for their ivory tusks continues.

Livestock, providing important sources of protein, can be integrated into a sustainable agriculture system. Many subsidized livestock practices that degrade lands, forests, and prairies gradually should be brought to an end. Education and training are needed to address the impact on human health and the environment of excessive consumption of meat in industrialized societies.

Free range grazing by an over-concentration of cattle and sheep, as well as by other animals such as goats, leaves the ground bare part of the year and thus subject to wind and water erosion. Domesticated varieties of cattle and sheep require constant human management and care in order to ensure a harmonious relationship with their habitat.

Pollution. In many areas the air is foul and the waters polluted. Sixty-five million tons of litter foul oceans and coasts.[9] In many countries untreated waste is routinely dumped in lakes and other freshwater bodies.

Air and water are essential resources for all living species. The pollution of these resources comes from industry and agriculture, from human garbage, or from overabundant and untreated animal and human waste. As population pressures increase so do pollutants expelled into the air and waters.

Urban and agricultural expansion creates pressures to drain swamps, fill in ponds, and block estuaries. These wetlands are precious. They act as reservoirs from which surface waters percolate down under the Earth's surface into aquifers to supply refreshing and life-giving water. Such a precious resource can be destroyed if each wetland, estuary, lake, or river is treated in isolation and polluted. It is important to understand and protect the totality of river systems, which do not follow or adhere to political boundaries.

Wetlands are also home to many species of bird, animal, and plant life. When wetlands are tampered with or destroyed, irreparable damage is done to those species. Fish can no longer hatch and grow in their natural environment. Birds can no longer nest and bring forth their young. In North America, the Chesapeake Bay, one of the world's richest marine habitats, is dying under its burden of development and damage from agricultural, industrial, and urban wastes.

It is ironic that modern economies—with an abundance of factories, power and industrial plants, and automobiles—threaten the quality of life. "Breathing in Bombay is now equivalent to smoking 10 cigarettes a day. In Mexico City, female diplomats are urged to return home during pregnancy, and in

Bangkok, where a million city residents were treated for respiratory problems in 1990, lung cancer is three times as common as in the rest of the country."[10]

Soviet authorities evacuated and destroyed towns around the town of Chernobyl, which received nuclear fallout from the meltdown at the Chernobyl nuclear reactor in 1989. American authorities had to evacuate Love Canal, New York, in 1980, when they found the environment in that community polluted by toxic wastes at levels far higher than humanly tolerable. Some two thousand people died as the result of a chemical gas leak at the Union Carbide Plant in Bhopal, India, in 1984. The ecological balance of Prince William Sound in Alaska was harmed by the multimillion gallon oil spill from the oil tanker Exxon Valdez in 1990. These disasters caused by pollution forecast a dire future.

Global Warming and Energy Usage. The world today faces an energy crisis. We depend on dwindling supplies of fuel, particularly oil and fuelwood. But the consumption of these fuels aggravates our plight by emitting gases into the atmosphere that affect the Earth's ecosystem.

The present dependence on oil as the world's largest energy source may seem to some people universal and inevitable. Yet it has only been in the past twenty to thirty years that the need for oil has become so great that some refer to its use as an addiction. In our day oil reserves have been depleted in North America, Australia, Asia, New Zealand, and western Europe. The Middle East has reserves estimated to last for 100 years, if they are used at 1991 production rates. Yet growing world economies may require 75 percent more energy in the next thirty years.[11]

At present, 26 percent of the world's oil comes from the Persian Gulf. If there is no change in energy policies, that figure would triple to nearly 70 percent, because two-thirds of the world's known oil reserves are in that area.[12] The Middle East, as the Gulf War of 1991 reminds us, is a very volatile region. Wars over oil have damaged both marine and terrestrial ecosystems and caused untold human suffering. Fluctuations in price caused by these wars have destabilized the economies of poorer nations around the world.

As petroleum becomes more and more expensive, the gap between the rich and the poor countries widens. A person in the United States currently uses an average of twenty-four barrels of oil per year, a person living in Europe uses twelve, and a person in sub-Saharan Africa uses one barrel per year. The appropriate level of consumption by the year 2030 (allowing for population increases, stretching out of the oil supply, and a reduction of the environmental impact of oil's use) should be an average of no more than 1.2 barrels per person per year.[13]

In developing countries people's lives are disrupted by the search for dwindling supplies of firewood. "Throughout the world, women are carrying loads up to 35 kilograms over distances as much as 10 kilometres from home."[14] What this does to women's health and energy can be imagined. Family nutrition declines. The source of the firewood cannot but dwindle, often leading to deforestation and desertification.

Many scientists warn of a possible catastrophic *global warming* effect, caused by the release of carbon dioxide (CO_2) into the atmosphere through fossil-fuel burning and through the cutting of trees (trees absorb carbon dioxide). Since industrial times carbon dioxide in the atmosphere has increased by 25 percent. Released carbon dioxide has a greenhouse-like effect, trapping heat from the sun that would otherwise radiate off the Earth.

Even small changes in the Earth's temperature can produce large effects: mean temperatures during the last Ice Age were only five degrees centigrade cooler than today. A doubling of 1860 levels of carbon dioxide concentrations could raise the Earth's mean temperature from 1.5 to 4.5 degrees centigrade, reaching the highest levels since the human species appeared on Earth.

This global warming process could create environmental and social disaster. Possible results include flooding of lowlands due to melting polar ice caps, substantial climate changes, and frequent flooding and drought brought about by changes in weather patterns. Forests, rangelands, and swamps could be traumatized.

For poor, subsistence farmers, particularly in lowland or coastal areas, such changes could spell catastrophe. "Over the long run fossil fuel use in industrial countries may be the most important determinant of the global poverty rate."[15] At the present rate of carbon dioxide growth, the conditions for such a disaster would be likely to occur in the middle of the next century.

After the world community decides to take action, it will require a generation or more to replace fossil fuels with other energy sources, to control deforestation, and to reforest. During that time, rising temperatures and drought may spread forest fires, which contribute more carbon dioxide to the atmosphere while depleting the forest that helps to remove it — a vicious cycle.[16] This is the grimmest scenario.

Fossil fuel use also creates *acid rain*. Acid rain results from the discharge of sulfur dioxide into the atmosphere by electric power plants, industries, automobiles, and every building that heats with coal or oil. (Many of these sources also discharge toxic metals that can cause cancer and birth defects.)

Scientists do not yet fully understand the chemical processes involved in acid rain's interactions with biologic ecosystems. Its effects, often demonstrated thousands of miles away from the pollutant source, are radical and seemingly irreversible; they occur with alarming speed.

The addition of large amounts of acid to lakes and freshwater ponds reduces and eventually eliminates their ability to sustain life. Hundreds of lakes are now lifeless. Acid rain causes mature forests to weaken and die. Such dying forests were first noticed in central and eastern Europe in 1972. The decline has spread to eleven tree species. People have detected dying forests in eastern North America, Latin America, the Caribbean, Africa, and parts of Asia. In Germany the Black Forest has lost one-third of its trees.

While some cities and nations have begun to curb their pollutants, others spew out increasing amounts of them. North America emits higher levels of carbon dioxide emissions than any other area. Yet should Europe, which emits the second highest, and Russia, the third, substantially reduce emissions, China may still neutralize all net gains. China plans to finance its economic expansion exclusively with coal, which emits the highest concentration of sulfur dioxide of all fossil fuels.

In October 1983 an enormous hole was discovered in the *ozone layer* above Antarctica. The ozone layer is one of the layers of the atmosphere that surrounds the Earth. It protects the Earth from the sun's ultraviolet radiation, which is harmful to living cells. In December 1988 a similar hole was discovered above the northern polar regions. In October 1991 the United States Government reported that the ozone layer above the United States was so thin that it exposed people residing in that region to higher levels of radiation than ever before. Scientific evidence released in late 1991 suggests that ozone depletion is far worse than previously estimated.[17]

The U.S. National Academy of Sciences warned in 1979 that as more ultraviolet radiation reaches the Earth, the incidence of human skin cancer will increase. We may, in reality, face even greater risks. Many agricultural scientists believe crop yields will be reduced by the solar radiation. Marine biologists fear the larvae of shrimp, crabs, and other important seafood species will be killed and micro-organisms at the base of the marine food chain destroyed.

What causes ozone depletion? A pollutant called chlorofluorocarbon (CFC) gases, emitted from spray cans, jet planes, and refrigeration and air conditioning units. These gases migrate to the stratosphere, one of the layers of the Earth's atmosphere. Once they reach the stratosphere, these pollutants, through a complex chemical interaction, diminish the ozone layer, allowing harmful ultraviolet radiation to penetrate to the surface of the Earth. Encouragingly, twenty-four nations agreed in Montreal in 1987 to achieve a 35 percent net reduction in worldwide CFC production by 1999, and subsequent agreements have encouraged countries to phase out CFCs. Even if these emissions are greatly reduced by the end of this century, deterioration of the ozone layer from prior emissions is likely to continue for decades.[18]

WARFARE AND THE ENVIRONMENT

One hundred and sixty armed conflicts have occurred since World War Two, most of them in developing countries. The rate is increasing. In 1950 nine conflicts began each year; now fourteen wars break out every year. Since World War Two sixteen million people, most of them civilians, have been killed.[19]

Warfare obviously is a great destroyer of the environment. Warfare causes environmental destabilization. We have only to picture the defoliation of trees caused by Agent Orange during the Vietnamese conflict or the degraded Kuwait shorelines following the Gulf War to acknowledge this fact. In Uganda and Nicaragua war refugees were forced onto marginal lands, destroying trees and ground cover in the process. Whole groups of refugees sometimes overtax the carrying capacity of land to such an extent that starvation and severe land degradation result, as in the Sahel. Warfare often weakens a nation's political structure, rendering it unable to address the environmental damage and human debilitation caused by the warfare.

Nuclear processes have caused severe environmental problems. The Chernobyl reactor meltdown contaminated animals, plants, and soil, as well as human beings. A number of groups of people around the world have been disenfranchised of their land and resources because their areas were used for nuclear testing or were close to nuclear power or armament plants. There are thousands of nuclear waste sites, created by the nuclear armament buildup. On and around these sites the contaminated soil, water, and air have affected the lives of many people, often indigenous peoples and people of color.

Shortages of resources contribute to the causes of wars. Although coalition leaders claimed the Gulf War was not fought over oil, it seems difficult to justify the war's momentum aside from the desire to keep this region open to oil trading. In the future more wars may be fought over another scarce resource — water.

The amount spent on armaments ($150 per world citizen,

$750 billion a year, or 6 percent of the global Gross National Product)[20] could solve many environmental problems. Indeed, developing nations have asked developed countries to spend .7 percent of their GNP (Gross National Product) in helping them with environmental problems. A diversion of military spending to other purposes could greatly aid us in attending to human health problems, cleaning up waterways, educating people about family planning, rehabilitating soil, and providing literacy training. Further, much technical expertise that now is devoted to military hardware development could be focused instead on research on sustainable technologies.

Preoccupation with national security helps people avoid the real national security issues: clean air and water, access to productive land, democracy and human rights, protection of viable ecosystems. It is these latter issues that, if they are not solved, create the potential for devastating warfare.

"FEELING" THE FACTS

What happens to us, to all of us, when faced in one way or another with the dangers to our planet?

First, we deny. Most of us feel numbed by suggestions of environmental deterioration. National leaders, spurred by powerful interest groups, deny the reality of our crisis today. In this century we have known nations to deny facts of inhumanity too horrible to contemplate.

If we stop denying, we grieve. Many of us can recall natural settings that are no more. Trees we loved are gone, rivers we fished or swam in are off-limits or unsafe for those who would enjoy them. What landscapes will our future generations see? We mourn the loss of what the Christian poet Gerard Manley Hopkins calls the "deep down freshness of things" when nature is paved over and built on. We begin to hear the cries of the animals. We mourn the loss of nature's visual beauty, sounds, and smells. Hopkins's poem "Binsey Poplars" expresses such grief:

My aspens dear, whose airy cages quelled,
Quelled or quenched in leaves the leaping sun,
All felled, felled, are all felled;
    Of a fresh and following folded rank
        Not spared, not one
        That dandled a sandalled
    Shadow that swam or sank
On meadow and river and wind-wandering wee-
winding bank.

O if we but knew what we do
    When we delve or hew -
Hack and rack the growing green!
    Since country is so tender
To touch, her being so slender,
That, like this sleek and seeing ball
But a prick will make no eye at all,
Where we, even where we mean

    To mend her we end her,
        When we hew or delve:
After-comers cannot guess the beauty been.
    Ten or twelve, only ten or twelve
        Strokes of havoc unselve
        The sweet especial scene,
        Rural scene, a rural scene,
        Sweet especial rural scene.[21]

If we grieve, as does Hopkins, then we can perhaps feel compassion — for the Earth, for all of us who must live on it, even
for God, who loves it so. We feel an empathetic connection to
the Earth, as does Hopkins, comparing the sudden destruction
of the human eye to the felling of the grove. When the U.S.
astronauts saw Earth from space — a tiny, azure sphere — the
seed ground of all that we love — they were overcome by compassion and love for it. We come to sense on a deep level — as
children do — that our destiny and that of the Earth are one.

SUGGESTIONS FOR INDIVIDUAL REFLECTION OR GROUP DISCUSSION

1. Reflect on the following questions:
   a. What are the most beautiful aspects of the environment in your region?
   b. What is a danger to the environment in your region?

2. Consider the following questions:
   a. What are we already doing to be good stewards of creation? How can we improve?
   b. Have we evaluated our own use of resources, such as gas, oil, water, light? How are we stewards in what we wear and eat?
   c. Are we willing to adjust our comfort level to save resources and provide for a more equitable distribution of these resources among all peoples?
   d. How can we help raise concern for creation among friends? Within government? Within the church?

3. Select one environmental issue that affects your community (such as global warming, air pollution, water contamination, species loss) and prepare a report about the problem and possible solutions. Organize a group to discuss, analyze, and develop a plan of action.

4. Write a story about how perceptions of environmental or social well-being have changed in your area or in the world during your lifetime. Encourage several older persons to participate. Share the stories. Create a prayer or symbol that expresses the group's understanding of the changes experienced and the meaning and consequences of these changes. Publish your stories in local media. Form pressure groups to protect or regenerate threatened local ecosystems.

CHAPTER 3

Indigenous People and the Earth

INDIGENOUS PEOPLE AND CHRISTIAN FAITH

A discussion of traditional indigenous people and their ties to the environment is appropriate, for at least three reasons. First, many have a deep sense of the sacred power of the Earth, and, no less important, they also have a remarkable capacity to live in harmony with the Earth. The contrast between the impact on the environment of their mode of living and that of modern industrial societies makes this clear.

Second, market-oriented development projects threaten these peoples today. Indigenous peoples are frequently victimized when such development projects are carried out without regard for ecological processes or the inhabitants of the area affected by the project. Colonists or developers often tend to view the ecological empathy of indigenous peoples as ignorant and backward, an impediment to human progress. Such was the case to a large extent with the European invasion of the North American continent. Natives who did not die from diseases brought by the conquerors were pushed off their lands and forced to live on marginal areas, in some cases far from their traditional hunting grounds. The same pattern is seen as the exploitation of rain forests, home to many indigenous peoples, is promoted in the interest of a global cash economy.

A third and, perhaps, most important reason for including a discussion of indigenous people here is that their disposition or attitude toward the natural world in which they are at home may help us to better recognize and restate Christian theological values in light of the environmental crisis. This does not mean, of course, that the Christian churches are arbitrarily to abandon long-held theological values or that there is not a shadow side to most cultures. But just as European Christianity learned much from classical antiquity, so we stand to profit greatly from the indigenous experience in living in harmony with the whole sacred community.

HOW AND WHY MANY INDIGENOUS PEOPLES LIVE SUSTAINABLY

There are societies of people in our world today who seem to be remarkably at ease in creation. The people who make up these societies have, almost invariably, lived in the same area for hundreds or thousands of years. They are the indigenous, tribal, or native people of the area.

There is a unique quality to their stance to nature. They stress above all else the need to maintain harmony with the natural world, a world enclosed within a more vast world, which is the cosmos.[1] Thus, all relationships to the natural world and all human activities take place within a world-view that teaches how the cosmos came into being and how it maintains its order. Human activities are to be in harmony with this order.

The content of native traditions differs radically from that of monotheistic religions. An important element of monotheistic religions is a consequence of a *Fall,* in which the harmonious ties that bind humankind and nature are shattered. It follows that there is something perpetually problematic about nature itself—to what extent it leads to God, to what extent it leads away from God. Historically, this very difficult problem has been simplified to criminal extremes by some well-intentioned Christians who insisted on an opposition between God and nature that the biblical texts do not justify. Further, monotheistic religions stress the covenant between human beings and God, lived out in a sacred history. The indigenous experience of religion has difficulty with this notion. What matters most in the indigenous perspective, the pivotal conviction, is the chaos that comes upon us when the harmony between nature and humans is in ruins.

Tradition plays a decisive part in the life of the people. The rituals that emerge from it are based on a sense of prohibitions and limits. Animals and plants are sacred. People and nature are bound together by mutual limits and prohibitions. The interaction of humans, animals, and plants has ritual meaning, but surprisingly an intimate and personal meaning as well, since indigenous people hear "voices" in the other sacred beings around them that guide them in living together for mutual benefit.

Indigenous people know the intricacies of the environment in the most intimate way. This is their rich culture, their heritage, which is passed on from generation to generation. With the wisdom of hindsight, we can now see how the Europeans in their first contact with these peoples dismally failed because their arrogance kept them from learning. Needless to say, there were numerous European observers who were quite aware of the effects of such pride and condemned it, and these voices that go from Dante to Montaigne to Las Casas should also be taken into consideration.

The indigenous peoples of our world continue to call out to us, joining their cry to that of the Earth, to bring the human species back into communion with nature. In their splendidly simple but effective ways they still offer insights and concrete help in learning how to live with nature. Some indigenous peoples teach what societies in industrialized countries have failed to grasp — that personal well-being, the common good, environmental health, and a community's spiritual life matter. Indigenous peoples do not experience gaps between the natural, the human, and the sacred. Through ritual, symbol, and dance, the cosmos, including daily human activity, is seen and lived out as a holy order. In this order human life is lived efficiently and well. The human burden upon the Earth can be lessened if we, like indigenous peoples, learn to meet our needs and desires by cultivating satisfying, sacred, harmonious relationships within ourselves, with the human community, and with the Earth.

The creation stories of indigenous peoples are the matrix for the peoples' cosmological, cultural, and social existence. In accord with these mythic statements, the cultural heritage of the group is completely interconnected with nature. The truly great society, many of these cultures recognize, is the society of the divine, the natural, and the human. An ethical life, imbued with the sacred mystery of relationship, supports full communion for all in existence.

Indigenous people have in common an understanding that there exists a pervasive mystery in the cosmos, a creative presence. While holding this understanding in common, indigenous cultures have varied voices, some of which speak in the remainder of this chapter. Just as biologists remind us that we need diversity in plant and animal life, so we need to hear varied cultural voices in order to enhance the well-being and the creative, sacred imagination of us all.

In *Make Prayers to the Raven*, Richard K. Nelson describes the sense of intimacy with the natural world in the perspective of the North American Indian:

> Examples to illustrate the interchange of meanings between Koyukon people and the surrounding land could be multiplied almost inexhaustibly. The terrain is permeated with different levels of meaning—personal, historical, and spiritual. It is known in its finest details, each place unique, each endowed with that rich further dimension that emerges from the Koyukon mind. Yet, as real and alive as this dimension is, it cannot be known except through the people whose lives and culture derive from this landscape. I do not mean to imply that such associations are unique to the Koyukon; I mean that the Koyukon homeland itself is unique because of the particular human imprint that it has embodied over the centuries.[2]

The destiny of the native peoples of the North American continent in a very deep and complex way is inseparable from the destiny of the North American land. Neither can be saved, or fully be alive, except in and through the other.

The Subanun people of the Philippines, another case in point, are one of the tribal groups who live in the northwestern sector of the Island of Mindanao. Their creation story reflects the intimacy that these people experience with nature. In their tradition the creative presence is named Apo Gumulang. Apo Gumulang is all-powerful and is master of the universe. Apo Gumulang had no beginning and is the giver of all life. Apo Gumulang was the Creator of the first man and woman, Aran and Eba. From these two descended all generations, all races, and all ages. The Subanun further relate that Apo Gumulang created all other things that we find in our world and in the heavens.

For the Subanun, the awesome creative presence within nature is mirrored in the praise of the *bal'yan*, the spirit intermediary between the Subanun people and the supernatural world, as he stands before the first tree to be cut for use in the sacred Subanun Thanksgiving Festival, *buklug*. The *bal'yan* begins his chant, calling upon the spirits who live in the tree and in the forest, the deities left behind by Apo Gumulang to protect his creation. The *bal'yan* calls upon Apo Gumulang, the Giver of Life and the Giver of All Things. He calls upon the tree itself, asking permission to cut the tree, helping the tree to give itself, singing the praise not only of the tree but also of the forest as a whole, and the Creator who designed it and who lives on in it.

Ancient ritual patterns and personal spiritual disciplines maintain relationships among people and between peoples and nature. All that had been diminished during the passage of the year is made new and full and vigorous at the annual new year or springtime festivals. The basic pattern of existence is experienced as movement and change contained within a seasonally renewed world.

On more familiar grounds, the early Hebrew people were

indigenous to harsh desert lands. In spite of the extreme conditions they faced, their religious stories reflect reverence for creation. They are warned against hoarding crops beyond the reach of wild animals and needy neighbors. The Hebrew writer of the Book of Deuteronomy contrasts the approach to farming in the new Promised Land, Canaan, with conditions remembered from Egypt. The most difficult part of farming in Canaan was not the physical labor but obedience to God and a moral responsibility toward intricate natural relationships:

> You shall love the Lord your God, therefore, and keep [God's] charge, . . . decrees, . . . ordinances, and . . . commandments always. Remember today . . . it is you who must acknowledge [God's] greatness . . . For the land that you are about to enter to occupy is not like the land of Egypt, from which you have come, where you sow your seed and irrigate by foot like a vegetable garden. But the land you are crossing over to occupy is a land of hills and valleys, watered by rain from the sky, a land that the Lord your God looks after. The eyes of the Lord your God are always on it, from the beginning of the year to the end of the year. If you will only heed [God's] every commandment that I am commanding you today—loving the Lord your God, and serving [God] with all your heart and with all your soul—then [God] will give you the rain for your land in its season, the early rain and the later rain, and you will gather in your grain, your wine, and your oil; and [God] will give grass in your fields for your livestock, and you will eat your fill (Deuteronomy 11:1-2, 10-15).

These words from Deuteronomy call to mind the relationship of the Native American Indians and the Subanun people to their lands, and of the Aymara Indians of the highlands of Bolivia to the natural rhythms of their environment. Yet, in discussing the similarities between the Hebrew religion and indigenous practices, we should not overlook the differences. They are similar in stressing harmony and the ethical imperative on humans—

based on a creation story—to respect and care for the land. They are different in that for indigenous peoples, the land does not have a God who watches over it. Rather, the mysterious, creative presence is *in the land* and all there is. Take, for example, the Navaho people. For them, the creative presence is the beautiful (*hozhooni*). *Hozhooni* is in everything. Humans need to enter into that beauty, be aware of it, honor it, acknowledge it:

> In the house of long life, there I wander.
> In the house of happiness, there I wander.
> Beauty before me, with it I wander.
> Beauty behind me, with it I wander.
> Beauty below me, with it I wander.
> Beauty above me, with it I wander.
> Beauty all around me, with it I wander.
> In old age traveling, with it I wander.
> On the beautiful trail I am, with it I wander.[3]

For the Subanun, as for other indigenous peoples, the link between cosmology and the creative mysterious presence in all is also lived out by them in sustainable environmental practices. Among the Aymara Indians the community determines what will be grown for the benefit of all. The community then tells farmers what crops to grow and regularly instructs them to leave an area fallow. This communal organization of agriculture ensures that an adequate diversity of crops is grown to meet the needs of the community. It gives food and some protected habitat for wild animals. It also gives the land sufficient time to rest and recuperate. If a family's land is to be fallow for a full year, the produce of the other members of the community provides for the needs of that family. As a result, the Aymara agricultural system has been in place for hundreds of years without depleting the soil.

The Aymara approach to agriculture is but one part of their communal life. They see all creation as one community. They strive constantly to keep creation in balance—the relation of humans to nature, the relation of humans to the "Extra-Human" or divine, the relation of nature to the divine. For the Aymara, any breakdown in the life of the community, any imbalance in the relationship of one part of the community to another, can bring disaster to all.

> We are told that the land is to be exploited as much as possible to become rich, be powerful, and rule over men. Instead, in our conception the land has to be fertilized, protected, respected, and venerated with offerings and sacrifices because it is she who gives us life. The land is not for exploitation, but to live from it from generation to generation.[4]

The communion of creation, exemplified in the Aymaran culture, is common to many indigenous people throughout the world.

The indigenous peoples of the Philippines have lived, and continue to live today, lifestyles in communion with the natural rhythms of the universe. The following account is recorded by Vincent Busch:

> There is a story of fishermen in Palawan that clarifies good work. They were given small boats and equipment by a businessman to fish for large tuna. He paid them 250 pesos for each tuna. They went out each week, caught two tuna and then rested. The businessman called them lazy because they could be earning much more money if they fished every day. The fishermen did not measure up to his definition of hard work. Such hard work would deplete the fishing grounds off Palawan. The fishermen were wise. Their work was good work because it safely conformed to the life cycle of their Palawan oasis.[5]

Those fishermen gave up wealth and comfort, and endured the wrath of the businessman, in order that their oasis could live.

Other indigenous peoples around the world join their Filipino, Bolivian, and North American brothers and sisters in teaching us how to live in communion with nature. C. Dean Freudenberger recalls the following from his experience as an agricultural development assistant in Zaire, then the Belgian Congo:

> I observed that the yields of corn in one of the fields we were working had fallen considerably. During a late afternoon a local villager saw me walking the rows of corn in an attempt to determine if there was an observable pattern to the decline . . .
> The villager took one look at the field and then looked at me. He said, "Things do not look very good." I agreed, and then I asked him for his advice about what needed to be done. He replied, "Go into the forest to see what it teaches." . . .
> The forest taught me that soils are very fragile. They can be cleared and planted to grain crops only at great risk and for very short periods of time before extensive loss is experienced . . . The forest teaches us of the intimate relationship of plant, animal, and micro-biological life within and upon the inorganic stuff which is foundational to the pattern of existence of the teaming life of this biotic community . . .
> The advice of my neighbor, one who never had the opportunity to learn to read or write, was the best advice I had ever received.[6]

The North American Indians reflect this sense of communion with the Earth in their distinction between "being" and "gaining." In his address to the Black Hills Alliance Survival Gathering, Russell Means in 1980 told those assembled:

> Europeans may see [Marxist materialism] as revolutionary but American Indians see it as simply more of that same old European conflict between being and gaining. Being is

40 Indigenous People and the Earth

a spiritual proposition. Gaining is a material act. Part of
that spiritual process was and is to give away wealth, to
discard wealth in order not to gain. Material gain is an
indicator of false status among traditional people while it
is the "proof that the system works" to Europeans.[7]

This sense of moral responsibility for the Earth is mirrored
in the life and stories of other American Indian tribes. Joseph
Bruchac records for us an event about Swift Eagle, a member
of the Apache nation. Swift Eagle used his sense of moral
responsibility to teach two young boys very important lessons
about the relationship of the human species to the rest of nature.
Bruchac recalls:

One day . . . Swift Eagle, an Apache man, visited some
friends on the Onondaga Indian Reservation in central
New York State. While he was out walking, he heard
sounds of boys playing in the bushes.
"There's another one. Shoot it!"
He found that they had been shooting small birds . . . a
chickadee, a robin and several blackbirds. The boys looked
up at him, uncertain what he was going to do . . .
"Ah," he said, "I see you have been hunting. Pick up
your game and come with me."
He led the boys to a place where they could make a fire
and cook the birds. He made sure they said thank you to
the spirits of the birds before eating them, and as they ate
he told stories. It was important, he said, to be thankful
to the birds for the gift of their songs, their feathers and
their bodies for food. The last thing he said to them they
never forgot—for it was one of those boys who told me
this story many years later: "You know, our Creator gave
the gift of life to everything that is alive. Life is a very
sacred thing. But our Creator knows that we have to eat
to stay alive. That is why it is permitted to hunt to feed
ourselves and our people. So I understood that you boys
must have been very, very hungry to kill those little birds."[8]

Finally, we hear the voice of the Kogi, a people living in the mountain jungle of Colombia and threatened by modern ways:

We are the Elder Brothers. We have not forgotten the old ways. How could I say that I do not know how to dance? But now they are killing the Mother [the Earth]. The Younger Brother [the ignorant and greedy one], all he thinks about is plunder. He is cutting into her flesh. He is cutting into her arms. He is cutting off her breasts. He takes out her heart. He is killing the heart of the world.[9]

The perception that all is sacred, as demonstrated by the above examples, is essential for human well-being. This does not mean that we must idolize and sanctify all indigenous peoples. Many of them have become mere peripheral adjuncts to the industrialized market economy societies in which they live. In some cases their way of life has become as destructive and burdensome to creation as that of the dominant society in their region.

Because of pressures on their land, some indigenous peoples have embraced cash economies, buying market goods, including food, and stripping their forests or land in order to do so. Some indigenous people have over the years turned to a "bridge" group to access the market. This may be another ethnic or tribal group, one more integrated with the wider society. In the American context, mestizos have played this role. The bridge group has a foot in both worlds — that of the indigenous peoples and of the outside market-oriented groups. While the bridge group may assist the indigenous people by providing cash and a market for their goods, they also may be exploitative. The interests of the bridge group are not served or only weakly connected to the importance of sustaining the culture and the environment of the indigenous people.

Indigenous peoples have recently seen themselves as speaking for the Earth to the world. Calling themselves the Voice of the Earth, they spoke for the world's 250 million indigenous people at the United Nations Earth Summit in Rio de Janeiro in June 1992. They identify the following problems as causing them great anguish: toxic chemicals leaking into rivers, rain forests being felled, traditional communities threatened by commercial exploitation and pollution, and the traditional hunter/gatherer way of life endangered everywhere. They call on governments to "adopt territorial guarantees to let indigenous people preserve their traditional way of life and the earth's biological diversity."[10]

CONFLICT BETWEEN INDIGENOUS PEOPLES AND "DEVELOPMENT"

Many indigenous people have been oppressed by colonizers coming into their lands. They have been pushed off their lands, enslaved, and decimated by diseases brought by the colonizers. Religious groups, accompanying the invading armies, often attempted to suppress indigenous cultures and convert them from their traditional ways of living a sacred life in harmony with their surroundings. Governments of nations that have grown up around them have seen these people as obstacles to national development goals and their lands as holding only economic value.

In the twentieth century indigenous people and their poor, nonindigenous countrymen and women have been the recipients of aid from development organizations or from their own or other governments. Sometimes this aid has perpetuated the view that indigenous traditions hold little value. Their culture destroyed, their land plundered, their value to the larger community ignored, many indigenous communities have given up and joined the majority in the plunder of the Earth.

So-called development programs often destroy not only the Earth, but also the economy of an indigenous subsistence society and the very way of life of the society itself. Subsistence societies in general follow sustainable economic practices. They impose minimal damage on the environment. In farming and harvesting they do not disturb the natural systems of regeneration in the region in which they live. These people, contrary to a prevalent view in so-called developed societies, may be the most developed. That is to say, the economy of their subsistence society is environmentally sustainable. The economy and the environment can support the people into the future.

In the Andes, the Agroecological Project of the University of Cochabamba (AGRUCO) was started in 1985.

The project has been working for the last six years in several Andean communities in the context of a small participatory research and extension programme. The research results have shown that the local knowledge is based on a profound understanding of the local ecology. The indigenous techniques applied in cropping and animal husbandry are living examples of sustainable agriculture. They also fit into the local social-economic-cultural context, resulting in a dynamic harmony between these different components ... Many of these techniques are traditional and, at the same time, they can be regarded as modern in the sense of a sustainable agriculture.[11]

The fate of the Aymara Indians has changed considerably because of one development program. The Bolivian government reacted negatively to the Aymara land-use system. The government bureaucrats understood the land as "wasted" because it was not used during fallow periods and imposed a new system that did not allow for fallow periods. They encouraged the farmers to grow cash crops for export to help the government pay the foreign debt. The new program relied heavily on petrochemical fertilizers.

The results of this development program are now clear. The program has succeeded in destroying the soil. It has also destroyed the economy of the Aymara people by breaking down one of the most effective community-based agricultural systems in the world. Missionaries living among these people have seen the contrast between the native system that has a strong land ethic and the imposed, greedy, and profit-oriented system that has replaced it. The churches have joined together with the people to respond to this situation, helping them to return to the more traditional economy. In so doing, the churches are giving a good example of a focused Christian land ethic leading to positive action in defense of the Earth.[12]

Sustainable development demands a whole new way of thinking on the part of those who wish to be a part of such development programs. The first change must be in the definition of *development*. The second change must be in the definition of the *poor*, who are to be developed.

Helena Norberg-Hodge first visited Ladakh in the early 1970s. A Himalayan people, the Ladakhs had been self-supporting farmers for thousands of years. Using organic wastes as fertilizer, recycling everything, the Ladakhs grew barley, wild flowers, and herbs. Over centuries they shared farm work, tools, and animals. Then, quite recently, the Indian government opened the area to tourism. Television and movies also entered into the life of the Ladakhs. Comparing their lives and belongings to those of the tourists and television images, the Ladakhs for the first time saw themselves as impoverished. Further, new government subsidies for imported grain made it cheaper for them to buy grain from the Punjab rather than from the nearest village. Some Ladakhs ceased to wear their traditional woolen clothing, replacing it with synthetic fibers. They have created mounds of garbage by using plastic and glass. Human waste is now a problem. Instead of being used as night soil to nourish the land, it is now flushed into new lavatories and septic tanks, using extra water and energy. Leaking sewage pipes recently raised the incidence of water-borne diseases. As their sense of security is lost, the Ladakhs have been destabilized, and there is increased conflict. In the early 1970s Ladakhan Tsewang Paljor said, "We don't have any poverty here"; in 1983, he said, "If you could only help us Ladakhis, we're so poor."[13]

To many people the word *development* means continued growth in an economy through which more and more things are made available for sale. True development, we believe, means perfecting the society to a point where it provides for its people the means to obtain *sufficient* food, shelter, clothing, health care, and education, within a culture that perceives life as meaningful, hopeful, and challenging, in an environment that the people protect. But what people see as sufficient varies from region to region, just as the web of life differs from ecosystem to ecosystem, and thereby all complexities begin.

Thus, the term *poor*, for many people, describes those who cannot afford to buy the many technological conveniences available to some in the more affluent societies. Such a concept of poverty is closely linked to the faulty concept of development discussed above. For others, poverty characterizes those societies that cannot provide for their people the means to acquire appropriate levels of food, shelter, clothing, health care, and education, or whose people lack a sense of meaning in their life, or who live in a depleted environment.

We distinguish between various orders of poverty. But what is perhaps most real and disturbing is the lack of any substantial give and take among cultures about what is to be considered essential in life. The fault perhaps lies largely in the industrial, technical, political aspects of modern western culture. Development need not bring indigenous people into conflict with the process of providing essential goods and services for their own or other communities. Neither does it need to bring the people into conflict with environmental rhythms. On the contrary, true development enhances the common sense, long experience, and traditional wisdom that have sustained indigenous people until the present time and allows other people to learn from it.

In the face of ecological destruction, indigenous peoples struggle to remain in communion with the Earth. Often their cause is to wage battle against the destroyers. We hear of the success of one man who tried to save his native land. Ole Letoluo retired to a barren area away from the city where he had lived most of his life. He wished to live out his days in the lands of his Maasai ancestors. For fifteen years he struggled to bring fertility back to the land. He restored the barren tract with hard work and great patience. If one were to walk that landscape today one would be hard-pressed to believe that it had been a barren, lifeless wasteland a short time before. A spring now flows from the hillside, and the women go there to draw their daily supply of drinking water. "We can now leave the river for the cattle," Letoluo reported. When asked where he had obtained the seed to replant the grass that now grew in abundance, his reply was, "God gave it to me." He went on to tell how he had "cut the grass species that he wanted before it started to drop the seeds, and laid the cut swaths on the ground in separate clumps." From those first clumps he repeated the process year after year, cutting and spreading and cutting again.[14]

This Maasai tribesman needed no modern technology. He needed no petrochemical fertilizers. He did not even need a barbed-wire fence to keep the wild animals away from his "desert reclamation" project. He needed faith in his communion with nature. He followed nature's ways, healing his portion of the face of the Earth.

SUGGESTIONS FOR INDIVIDUAL REFLECTION AND GROUP DISCUSSION

1. What experiences, if any, have you had with indigenous peoples? Did they reflect some of the views expressed in this chapter?

2. It may be difficult for some to sense the differences between the attitude toward the Earth of indigenous peoples and other religious perspectives. The prayers below have been written to convey some of the differences.[15] These prayers may be used on the occasion of a party celebrating the graduation of a student from school (in this example, Inday is graduating from agricultural school). Read the prayers aloud. Discuss the differences between them. With which prayer do you feel more comfortable? Why? What conclusions do you draw from comparing these two prayers?

PRAYER OF THE EARTH COMMUNITY

We thank you God, our nurturing Mother on Earth, for the many opportunities we have to enhance the Earth community today. We are grateful for Inday's ability to listen to and to learn from all things that interact to nurture the fertility of the soil and community. We pray that she may continue to live in harmony with the natural world. Bless her family, whose concern for the soil has taught her the wisdom of living lightly on the Earth. Guide her to use that wisdom to promote the health, fertility, and diversity of all beings here and throughout the Philippine archipelago. Lastly, we thank you for the food and the solidarity we share with all creatures. We pray for all who are denied a nurturing habitat. Guide us to appreciate in a mutually supportive way the life-enhancing role of every being so that all things can join the liturgy of all creation in praising You. Amen.

PRAYER OF THE MODERN WORLD

We thank you God, our almighty Father in heaven, for the many things that satisfy our needs in the modern world today. We are grateful for the culmination of Inday's professional course of studies enabling her to make the soil more productive and profitable.

We pray that she may find gainful employment. Bless her family who, through hard work and self-denial, saved the money for her professional training. Guide her to use her technical expertise to help industry and commerce flourish and to increase salaried employment for the human beings of our place and of our nation. Lastly, we thank you for this food and the solidarity we share with the people around us. We pray for people who do not have enough to eat. Guide us to steward carefully and to distribute fairly all things among human beings so that all people can enjoy the riches of the Earth and give You praise. Amen.

3. In what ways can you foster the life of indigenous peoples?

4. What elements of the world-view of indigenous peoples would you like to affirm in your own life? How will you do so? How will that modify your relationships with God, family and friends, nature?

CHAPTER 4

WHAT WENT WRONG?

THE ENLIGHTENMENT AND THE RISE of INDUSTRIALIZATION

There is no underestimating the impact of modern western values throughout the world. Many of these values originated in the Age of Reason. Its dominant traits, empiricism and scientific method are still with us today.[1]

There is, however, a reverse side to these achievements. Some thinkers have traced the general neglect of natural processes in the modern development of western civilization.[2] Other observers have pointed out that perspectives developed during the Enlightenment period have become unconscious assumptions in western culture. This is to say that Christians cannot change their way of dealing with nature without examining such assumptions.

Enlightenment as human awakening, as the discovery of the human potential for global transformation, and as the realization of the human desire to become the measure and master of all things is still the most influential moral discourse in the political culture of the modern age; for decades it has been the unquestioned assumption of the ruling minorities and cultural elites of the developing countries, as well as the highly industrialized nations ...

The Enlightenment mentality fueled by the Faustian drive to explore, to know, to conquer, and to subdue persisted as the reigning ideology of the modern West.[3]

A Christian response to today's social and environmental crises calls for examination of western Enlightenment values. Is the seventeenth century redeemable? Are its contributions faithful to biblically based Christian theology and helpful to Christianity as it responds to the degradation of creation?

THE ENLIGHTENMENT PERIOD

In terms of intellectual history, the great precursor is René Descartes, the mathematician and philosopher, with his mechanistic view of nature. His near contemporary Francis Bacon emphasized experimentation, followed by induction, followed by experimentation. Bacon's aim was to exert power and control over nature. Isaac Newton systematized with genius these intuitions. He stressed matter and nature as collections of machines or objects. Thomas Hobbes, turning to the political implications of this approach, concluded that humans are "self-moving systems of matter in motion,"[4] basically selfish and competitive, who maximize their self-interest economically. In economics, Adam Smith argued that the economic system, running on its own, with little government interference, would benefit the whole society.

These values of individualism and free markets, basic to the establishment of American democracy, had a dark side. Neither justice nor environmental awareness is a product of unbridled individualism.

Some flaws are obvious. First, God, the Creator, is hopelessly distant in this system. Having set the world in motion, God watches as people, who are now the center of the universe, pursue only their own self-interest.

Second, the sacred disappears in the material world.

Third, humans are reduced to competing individuals, not participants in a larger human or Earth community. Individual rights are more important than obligations to other humans or the created world.

Fourth, "my" growth in wealth will benefit "you," because it enriches society as a whole. This leads to a simplistic notion of "wealth trickling down."

Fifth, the function of nature is to be consumed or refashioned to create "wealth" used by humans.

Sixth, areas of life are no longer considered as complementary but contraries: lower/higher, public/private, government/economic system, mind/matter, spirit/matter, individual/community, rich/poor, owners/laborers, God/human beings, developed/undeveloped, and nature/God. Much of the conflict that we experience in today's world is and has been provoked by an acceptance of these opposites.

What, then, did the new worldview [the] Enlightenment accomplish? To begin with, it totally changed people's image of their place in the universe. From being servants of God (whatever their worldly station) each contributing to the life of His Church on Earth, they became isolated, competing agents. Human nature, once made in the image of God and innately capable of brotherly love, became a self-centered consumer of pleasure, the sole purpose of whose Reason was to further its own existence. If an image of God still lurked in human nature, it was one of omnipotence rather than compassion. Purpose in life shifted from serving God and society, and thereby oneself, to serving oneself first, and thereby — almost by accident — society. Fulfilling one's own desires became the most legitimate goal of existence. Where the God-given right of an individual to exist once put the other members of society under an *obligation* to care for her or him, in the new worldview no such social obligations are assumed. Each person has a *natural right* to preserve his life . . .

Finally, if God exists, the new worldview decrees that He speaks only through each individual's conscience, never through religiously ordained social laws. Nevertheless, worldly success, particularly material success, probably indicates divine approval and is a sign of great moral virtue. Entrepreneurs and corporate heads who create a means of livelihood for others are natural pillars of society. And those at the bottom, since they lack the necessary moral virtue, deserve their fate.[5]

ENLIGHTENMENT VALUES AND THE MODERN WORLD

The views just described helped shape modern industrial society, which began in England in the late eighteenth century. When we picture industrial development, we may see in our mind's eye factories, pollution, and people toiling at mechanical tasks. We may also envision people who have the security of paychecks and health benefits. We may picture the many products of industry, without which it is hard to conceive of modern society.

Industry has, indeed, given much to some people. It has been spectacularly successful, making great strides in alleviating want. At its best it is dynamic and adventuresome.

Industrialization and modern economies have also taken much. They make it difficult to set limits to growth; they exploit the weak; they unrestrainedly and systematically create environmental degradation.

COLONIALISM

Colonialism played a varying role in the history of Europe and the United States. Centuries after the Age of Exploration many parts of the world were colonized by the West. "As the Western nations assumed the role of innovators, executors, and judges of the international rules of the game defined in terms of competition for wealth and power, the stage was set for growth, development, and exploitation."[6] France, England, Belgium, Germany, Spain, and Portugal extensively colonized peoples around the world. There were some high ideals, but most were never actualized. Exploitation became rampant. Pride, greed, oppression of women, children, men, and nature, and genocide are among the evil aspects of colonialism. As industrialization grew, colonialism provided the source of raw materials. Eventually countries with varied, self-sufficient economies, based on tribal custom and the exchange of foodstuffs and other goods, were encouraged or forced to rely on a few cash crops, a new money exchange, and a dependency on the colonizers. People in the dependent, colonialized countries often came to rely on a single crop for cash. As the poor gave up their land for cash crops, they resorted to shifting cultivation on marginal lands, causing land degradation.

In many colonized countries an internal hierarchy (with a local elite at the top) developed. On the bottom were the poor. Their cultural values shifted and became confused because of the imposition of new ways and new values by the colonizers.

INDUSTRIALIZATION

The values of modern industrialized countries seem strange or even abnormal to other times and other cultures. Modern industrialization even clouded some of the original positive values of the Enlightenment.

> The idea of competitive market or free enterprise, in Adam Smith's sense . . . has never been fully implemented as a political or economic institution. In fact, the exponential growth of the central government, not to mention the ubiquity of the military bureaucracy, in all Western democracies has so fundamentally redefined the insights of the Enlightenment that self-interest, expansion, domination, manipulation, and control have supplanted seemingly innocuous values such as progress, reason, and individualism.[7]

Industrialization may to some extent be characterized by the notions of efficiency, technology, spiritual poverty, and globalization.

Efficiency. Efficiency means producing goods and services with the least possible expense in terms of money, energy, or time. It is marked by organization. Efficiency, without which a modern economy does not develop, takes into account only what carries a price tag. Clean air, clean water, fertile soil, all of which are encroached upon by industrial activities, are given no monetary value; therefore the economy freely and easily disposes of them.

Technology. Industrial society is also based on technology. New technologies help us to master nature and create products.

In this analysis, the difference between socialism and capitalism in industrialized societies is minimal. The two systems differ in the relation of the individual to the system. Both systems focus on material goods and economic growth, and both, unless modified, ignore the physical, natural processes on which the economies are actually based.

Industrial societies and technologies tend to respond positively to what grows, what is complex, and what is costly. This phenomenon creates social and environmental impacts that are diffuse, difficult to quantify, and nearly impossible to anticipate. New high-cost technology also widens the gap between the rich and the poor in developed countries.

A combination of need, desire, and advertising stimulates the appetite to buy, leading to economic growth. Advertising of consumer products may have some positive values, yet it does little to advance social well-being and environmental health. Advertising twists facts, human frustrations, and human needs and covers them with a potent but cloudy message closing us all in a prison of consumerism. The basic human needs for belonging, for spiritual inspiration, for acceptance are subtly woven into advertising images. Ads for some products play on human anxieties. A radio advertisement in the United States said that many scientists believed the fires set off in Kuwait during the Gulf war would create global *cooling* (not warming). The ad recommended that hearers buy winter sportswear! Such an ad confuses issues and manipulates people.

The search for markets constantly leads into new frontiers.

The countries colonized by European nation-states, and the American western frontier, were the first frontiers. Another frontier is technology, resulting in schemes to colonize space and in research in biotechnology. The final frontier may be the stake that future generations have in a healthy Earth.[8]

Spiritual Poverty. The industrial society has brought benefits to humans, for example, in medical advances, which help to prolong life expectancy. Yet it has worked to deprive human beings of an emotionally and physically satisfying way of life. It has helped to generate, in the late twentieth century, a sense of meaninglessness, a disbelief in social institutions, cynicism, and, as though to balance this, an intense demand that each person's rights and wants be fulfilled. It does so because it inherently tends toward destruction of nature and human social bonds.

Modern societies make it very easy to develop undesirable personal qualities—flattery, fear, envy, and desire. We are tempted to substitute these for joy, receptivity, compassion, sharing. We have little sense of being part of the world, of the Earth community. At the same time, we lose respect for otherness. We do not value other species or the ways in which other humans live their lives. In the end, we have no capacity to contemplate the paradoxical otherness and nearness of God.

Globalization. Modern industrialized nations, just like earlier colonial powers, seek to replicate their way of life in developing countries. The leaders of many developing countries then adopt their goals. Brazil's recent history exemplifies this process.

Brazil is perhaps one of the wealthiest countries in the southern hemisphere. It is a major exporter of coffee, orange juice, soy beans, sugar, cattle, cocoa, and corn. Brazil produces and exports these cash crops to meet payments on the foreign debt incurred by its military government to spur industrialization.

Over the past twenty years, Brazil has declared the intention of becoming a world power by the end of the century. Brazil's economic leaders have based their plan of development on the examples of industrial countries. These economic leaders have exploited natural resources, developed a broad industrial base, sought cheap labor, and aggressively courted world markets, particularly military ones. They also borrowed money in the 1970s to such an extent that in recent times Brazil has had to declare a moratorium on debt payment.

Such "development" has huge social and economic costs. In 1983 the Brazilian per capita income in U.S. dollars was $2,500, but 10 percent of the Brazilian population earned as much as the other 90 percent combined. Since 1983 poverty has deepened. Forty percent of those who are working are being paid less than the minimum wage. Even at minimum wage, a laborer works 3.5 hours for a gallon of milk, 8.2 hours for a pound of meat. In 1985, 40 percent of the Brazilian population was malnourished.[9]

This model of economic development has led to incursion into and misuse of the vast Brazilian rain forests. Mega-projects paid for by the government and industrial investors have driven small farmers off their meager landholdings so that lands can be used for corporate farming and ranching. Two hundred thousand migrants began an onslaught on the forest. Their slash-and-burn agriculture was inherently pointless. Within four years 80 percent of the settlers had to seek new land in other areas because of the poor soil beneath the felled rain forest. In the Brazilian state of Rondônia alone, an area the size of Germany, 30 percent of the forest has been denuded and left barren.

Some of the poorest farmers work as gold miners. They live in dire poverty in the wild-cat camps scattered throughout the forest wilderness. Mining companies were seen by some as heroic, because they created jobs for the poor. Their efforts have made Brazil one of the world's largest gold-producing countries. Some companies have operated without government control in feudalistic systems, which have given little economic return to those who actually bring the precious metal out of the earth. Their operations have polluted rivers with mercury and have caused armed confrontation with resident Indian tribes.

Brazil spent $34,000 on each industrial job it has created, $63,000 for each ranching job. This financial support is short-sighted and wasteful. Most of the projects have not become profitable, while the forest, which could be sustainably managed, has been destroyed. Today Brazil staggers under the burden of the huge foreign debt incurred in the financing of these unprofitable programs. That burden weighs heavily on the poor of Brazil, while the interest on that debt is paid each year into the banks of the richer nations. Those nations receiving the payments are the very nations that have profited from the natural resources of the Brazilian earth (such as beef from cattle ranches) and the labor of the Brazilian poor.

CONCLUSION

It is important that environmental and human devastation facing almost every country be seen in these wide contexts. Negative western values stemming from the Enlightenment need to be supplemented or replaced by those we find in Christianity, other faith traditions, and indigenous cultures around the world. The values we need now include a sense of community, responsibility for others and for the Earth, a sense of sacredness in the world, a deep valuing of aspects of life other than material goods. The environmental crisis, social injustice and poverty, and spiritual crises may yet pull us up short and lead us to question the path we have taken in the past two hundred years. Christians can embrace this challenge and bring moral and ethical pressures to bear on religious, political, and economic leaders to bring forth a new creation. The ways in which we can do so are the themes of the next three chapters.

SUGGESTIONS FOR INDIVIDUAL REFLECTION OR GROUP DISCUSSION

1. Was this discussion of the Enlightenment/colonialism helpful? Do you agree? Disagree? Why?

2. What are benefits of technologies that you use? Do you have any concerns about those technologies?

3. Has your country benefitted from modernization/industrialization? How? What have been some of the costs?

4. A Group Exercise: The Web of Life[10]
   a. Prepare a list of living and non-living things that belong to your habitat.
   b. Write the names of these things on 8.5″ x 11″ pieces of paper, a different name for each piece of paper. Write small.
   c. Give each participant one piece of paper.
   d. Ask each participant to draw the thing named on the piece of paper he or she received. A simple drawing is sufficient. Have crayons or pencils available.
   e. When the drawings are finished (allow about five minutes) ask the participants to pin their drawings to their shirt front or dress so the drawings can be easily seen.
   f. After all have attached their drawings ask the group to sit in a circle.
   g. Ask each participant to tell the life story of the thing that he or she drew. That life story should contain the real joys, fears, needs, and living conditions of the thing. Ask everyone to listen carefully to each life story.
   h. When everyone has shared ask the group to stand and look at the drawings. Ask the participants to find those things in the group which are connected in some way to the thing which they drew.
   i. Ask participants to go to the center of the circle and to hold onto those people whose drawings have some connection to the life story of their drawing. (For example, a person who drew a fish might hold onto a person who drew the sea.) Allow enough time for all participants to find and hold as many people as are connected to the life story of their drawing.
   j. When everyone is connected to other things ask the group to return to their seats.
   k. Ask the participants to share their feelings about their experience. Some guide questions are:
      (1) How did you feel?
      (2) Whom did you hold? Why?

     (3) Who held onto you?

     (4) Were you surprised at who related to you?

  l. Then ask the group how the things they drew would be affected by modernization or industrialization.

  m. Tell how the insights gained from this experience contrast with those of the Enlightenment thinkers and those that underlie the modern industrial and technological world.

CHAPTER 5

The Scriptural View of the Earth and Its Peoples

There is some controversy concerning the biblical tradition with respect to the environment. How do we explain environmental problems in Christian lands? The question brings up many knotty issues. Have Christians in the past consistently adhered to scriptural teachings? That question answers itself. Have other cultural values, principally those of the Enlightenment, provided a tinted glass through which Christians view a now dimmer scriptural teaching? Can concerned Christians today discern such alien values, helping us to reexperience nature and ourselves? Will the human species—created for freedom and charity—find the strength to rediscover scriptural insights and implement them?

Because Christians have not fully lived according to the biblical vision and may not have even seen it clearly, the need is to "gird our loins" and do battle against malevolent powers.

GOD AS CREATOR AND SUSTAINER

In the beginning was God.

There is no end to the depths alluded to in these words, nor can we put a limit to what that statement means to different peoples in different climes. Still, the majority of believers of the Jewish and Christian traditions hold that the statement means that God brought time itself into being and that in time we bear our greatest responsibilities.

The biblical creation story looks at the Earth through the eyes of faith. Scripture proclaims that the Creator and the created are bonded in peace and love. Out of love God gives this wondrous creation to humans as a gift, a heritage to be handed down, generation to generation. Creation is perpetual and unending.

To look upon creation as a gift from God is to feel how precious each particle of soil is, each mineral, each element of the Earth's bounty. We then affirm the meaning and dignity of the life of every creature, every species of plant and animal. In accepting creation as a blessing from the Creator Christians fully understand the meaning and dignity of human life. Finally, in accepting the gift of creation, we sense with joyfulness and pain the call to us to be co-creators with God, to give our life energies to enhance this world.

The biblical creation story opens with a vision of darkness, wind, and water: "The earth was a formless void and darkness covered the face of the deep, while a wind from God swept over the face of the waters" (Genesis 1:2). Out of the Creator's energies the elements emerge. Formless matter takes form. The Creator fills the void with land and water (Genesis 1:6-10). The Lord inaugurates creation with power: "Then God said, 'Let there be light'; and there was light. God saw that the light was good" (Genesis 1:3). Again and again, act by act, the Creator spoke and it happened; the Creator fashioned. And all that God created stood firm.

The awesome creativeness of God, however — and this is even more mysterious — does not strip nature of the liberty of response. The Bible portrays the third day as a day in which the newly formed Earth begins to express itself in response to God's creative intention. The creatures called forth by the Creator, though still vulnerable and dependent, form responsive relationships with one another!

God says, "Let the earth put forth vegetation" (Genesis 1:11). And so it does. The Earth provides for vegetation a home, as well as nutrients for life and health. The vegetation, in turn, returns nutrients to the soil and also protects the soil from the wind, rain, and sun. The rain, in its turn, provides life-giving water to the vegetation. The vegetation returns water, in the form of vapor, to the air, building up the moisture needed for the rain cycle. The air provides a medium to carry pollen, necessary to the fruit production process of many plants. The plants clean the air of carbon dioxide and, through the process of water evaporation, cool the air. So intricate and so elaborate is this system of responsive relationships, given by God's love, that scientists of today are still unlocking its secrets.

And so it was the Lord created multitudes of birds to "fly above the earth across the dome of the sky" as well as fish and sea creatures "with which the waters swarm" (Genesis 1:20, 21), and all of the other animals. In the biblical creation story the Creator felt increasing delight in the many creatures brought to life. Each of these creations played a role in the unfolding drama of this dynamic universe. Each creation was an intimate part of the whole. The relationships were such that there was no excess, no waste. The excess of one creation filled the need of another. The waste of one creation nourished another. God saw that it was "good" (Genesis 1:12). Creation mirrored that goodness of the Creator in the responsive relationships of all species.

God's delight in the diversity of nature shines through the stately repetitions of the first chapter of Genesis. The Lord called the dry land Earth, and the waters that were gathered together he called Seas. And God saw that it was "good" (Genesis 1:10). "The earth brought forth vegetation . . . And God saw that it was good" (Genesis 1:12). "God made the wild animals of the earth of every kind, and the cattle of every kind, and everything that creeps upon the ground of every kind. And God saw that it was good" (Genesis 1:25). The Creator's delight in the created world was so great that God proudly paraded all of Creation before the first human being. "So out of the ground the Lord God formed every animal of the field and every bird of the air and brought them to the man to see what he would call them" (Genesis 2:19).

These creatures were not puppets dangling from the Creator's fingers. The Creator proudly "loosed the bonds of the swift ass" (Job 39:5) to let the ass roam freely. The Creator brought creatures forth and gave each the capacity to live from its own initiative, however critical their dependence upon other creatures and their environment.

We see God's sustaining power of creation in these responsive relationships. The creative power of God gave sustaining power to the Earth, and the Earth responded. The Earth produced vegetation: the various kinds of seed-bearing plants and the fruit trees with the seed inside, each corresponding to its own species. In our day, we know that each seed is genetically coded with the whole history of that species from the time of its creation. Each seed also has within it the ability to reproduce again and to pass on the history and the future of the species. But that future cannot exist if the responsive relationships of soil, air, water, animal, and vegetable life forms are not lively and healthful.

The Creator's first loving word to creatures is a word of blessing and encouragement: "Be fruitful and multiply and fill the waters in the seas, and let the birds multiply on the earth" (Genesis 1:22). God creates in love and communicates love to all creatures. In their own way the creatures respond. God's relationship with all creatures, plants, animals, and humans continues to be most intimate.

In the Book of Job, the writer makes clear that human knowledge cannot begin to compare to the Creator's intimacy with creatures:

> "Can you hunt the prey for the lion,
>   or satisfy the appetite of the young lions
> when they crouch in their dens,
>   or lie in wait in their covert?
> Who provides for the raven its prey,
>   when its young ones cry to God,
>   and wander about for lack of food?

"Do you know when the mountain goats give birth?
Do you observe the calving of the deer?
Can you number the months that they fulfill,
    and do you know the time when they give birth,
when they crouch to give birth to their offspring,
    and are delivered of their young?
Their young ones become strong, they grow up in the
        open;
    they go forth, and do not return to them.

"Who has let the wild ass go free?
Who has loosed the bonds of the swift ass,
to which I have given the steppe for its home,
    the salt land for its dwelling place?
It scorns the tumult of the city;
    it does not hear the shouts of the driver.
It ranges the mountains as its pasture,
and it searches for every green thing."
                        (Job 38:39—39:8)

The Creator has a personal connection with all species of
natural life. Without the eyes of faith some modern humans see
predation, reproduction, and adaptation in an ecosystem of
mutual support. Hebrew writers, on the other hand, see the Lord
feeding the lion and the raven, serving as midwife for the successful birth of the fawn, and freeing the ass for life in the
wilderness.

Christians need not apologize for the ancient, nonscientific
perspective presented in the creation story. We can appreciate
how environmental systems express the intention of the Creator.
God not only created but also bestowed creativity upon the
Earth. Earthly life is creative, with inner resources and dependence as well. Each creature can respond to other creatures and
to the Creator. The Creator is a participant in the life of the
world; God is not passive nor remote.

The Creator did not fashion a spectacular display of objects
to confirm the power and might of the Creator. Nor was this

great array fashioned merely as a decorative backdrop against which the human drama was to unfold. The Creator made an Earth, lively and life-giving. The Earth has a great diversity of creatures, each portraying some part of the reality and goodness of the Creator.

CALL TO HUMANS TO IMAGE GOD TO ALL CREATION

The Bible, needless to say, offers no scientific explanation of the creation. The Bible does point out, however, the stance proper to our dealing with all other creatures. Scripture abounds with celebrations of creatures that are unique and vital, yet dependent upon other creatures, the environment, and God. The need for one another guides us in our caring.

The Psalms praise the Creator as the One who sustains what we now call the earthly ecosystem, the web of life:

> You make the springs gush forth in the valleys;
>   they flow between the hills,
> giving drink to every wild animal;
>   the wild asses quench their thirst.
> By the streams the birds of the air have their
>   habitation;
>   they sing among the branches.

> The trees of the LORD are watered abundantly,
>   the cedars of Lebanon that he planted.
> In them the birds build their nests;
>   the stork has its home in the fir trees.
> The high mountains are for the wild goats;
>   the rocks are a refuge for the coneys.

> O LORD, how manifold are your works!
>   In wisdom you have made them all;
>   the earth is full of your creatures.
>   (Psalm 104:10-12, 16-18, 24)

The Creator is indeed the One who sustains creation. The biblical creation story, however, goes further, telling us what modern experience has confirmed: to survive and flourish nature depends on us. The creation story of Genesis tells us:

> So God created humankind in his image,
> in the image of God he created them;
> male and female he created them (Genesis 1:27).

We cannot sound the depths of the notion of "in the image of God," but certainly it suggests that we mirror the Creator's care for creation. We are *more* responsive, *more* creative than other creatures, and our capacity for conscious choice gives us a unique responsibility. Does this mean that we are called to have dominion and power over all creation as the Creator does? We are indeed so called. We find that call in the next verses of Genesis:

> God blessed them and God said to them, "Be fruitful and multiply, and fill the earth and subdue it; and have dominion over the fish of the sea and over the birds of the air and over every living thing that moves upon the earth." God said, "See, I have given you every plant yielding seed that is upon the face of all the earth, and every tree with seed in its fruit; you shall have them for food" (Genesis 1:28-29).

The closeness of the verses is striking. One verse, Genesis 1:27, proclaims the human species to be made in God's image. The other, Genesis 1:28-29, proclaims the dominion of the human species over creation. Their closeness helps us to understand that our power over creation, our dominion over the Earth is like that exercised by the Creator. It is limited by the limits that the Creator put upon the power and dominion exercised in the loving creative act.

In the act of creation there is no autocratic authority. The Creator is self-giving; the created responds. The Creator provides for the freedom, the shelter, and the food for the birds of the air and the fishes of the sea and all the other living things. We, too, imaging the Creator to the created world, must provide for the freedom and the welfare of our fellow human beings and for all creation.

In creating, the Creator gives unstintingly. We must mirror that unselfishness. In creating, the Creator showed boundless love. In our relationship to the created world we should participate in that love. We must reflect God's understanding of the creatures, as did Adam when he named them. The words of scripture in the creation story of Genesis (1:1-2:3) and in the speech of the Lord to Job (Job 38-39) call out to us to show compassion for creation. The psalms urge us to be stewards of the Earth (Psalm 104). They call out to us to take into account the whole of creation, not just the good of the human species. A morally sound, interdependent creation mirrors the love and goodness that the Creator exhibited toward it. Our role is to support such interdependence, out of love of God.

A HOLY PEOPLE ON A HOLY LAND

The Hebrew people accepted their designation as chosen people of God. This conviction, this faith in God, gave them the strength to free themselves from the slavery they suffered in Egypt. God's intention, however, was not merely to free and form a holy people but also to liberate a land, which would become holy in the sight of the people. Their deliverance from bondage and poverty was to be fulfilled in their enjoyment of and care for the new land promised them.

When the Hebrew slaves came forth from Egypt, they were tried and tested for many years before entering the Holy Land. During that time, they become a New People. They now understood the value of a fertile land. At Sinai, God gives this New People a vision of a new way of living. In ten simple precepts, spoken through the wisdom of Moses, the Creator sets forth a vision that the people must follow if they wish to remain holy and in the holy land.

The Ten Commandments embody a vision of justice for human society. That vision of justice is based on the Hebrew belief that there is but one God, the Creator of all and the Giver of life, who executes justice for the oppressed (Psalm 146:5-7). The one God gives sufficient bounty to the Earth. All people can coexist, sharing in the fruits of the creation while having sufficient energy to harvest and time for rest. Those who follow the ten precepts will enjoy both the bounty and the freedom given by the Creator.

The biblical story expands the vision of justice to include a vision of justice for nature. Each species has its own place in creation, its own needs and purposes. The one God knows and respects all creatures, lovingly providing sustenance and time for rest for all the inhabitants of the Earth. The Sabbath Laws, recorded in Exodus 20:8-11, govern the Sabbath, a day of rest for all people and all livestock. In Exodus 23:10-12 these laws are expanded to govern nature as well: "For six years you shall sow your land and gather in its yield; but the seventh year you shall let it rest and lie fallow."

This new vision of justice culminates in a covenant between the Creator and the created. The Creator's claim to the land prevails. The land is removed from politics to the realm of ethical decision: "For the land is mine; with me you are but aliens and tenants" (Leviticus 25:23). Rights of tenancy become a sacred, religious concern, with such rights shielded from politics and economic manipulation. The promised land is thus drawn within the circle of ethical reflection at the very heart of Hebrew faith.

Since the promised land was an object of moral concern, human obligations to the landscape and to other creatures who lived there are recognized. At the greatest breadth of their reflection, the Hebrews struggled to appreciate what it meant to serve a God who was not a tribal deity tied to a particular landscape: "Indeed the whole earth is mine" (Exodus 19:5). They tried to appreciate the claims of all animals, domestic and wild, who shared the land with them:

O LORD, how manifold are your works!
In wisdom you have made them all;
the earth is full of your creatures (Psalm 104:24).

BIBLICAL UNDERSTANDING OF POLLUTION:
THE PROPHETS

Pollution is a biblical term that conveys God's disgust at the moral fouling of human relationships and the impact of social degradation upon God's beloved Earth. In our day the word *pollution* depicts environmental contamination. The prophets obviously lacked our scientific knowledge, but they were highly sensitive to the interactions that knit the human community to the natural landscape and the divine purpose.

The prophets saw that pollutants, entering the sensitive web of life at one point, spread quickly through the whole. Although concerned about the impact of pollution upon human welfare, they were equally concerned about God's honor and the health of the landscape.

The earth dries up and withers,
    the world languishes and withers;
    the heavens languish together with the earth.
The earth lies polluted
    under its inhabitants;
for they have transgressed the laws,
    violated the statutes,
    broken the everlasting covenant.
Therefore a curse devours the earth,
    and its inhabitants suffer for their guilt.
                                    (Isaiah 24:4-6)

In the biblical concept of our relationship to nature, the Earth participates in a mysterious way in the consequences of sin. The Hebrew people initially had no concept of heaven or hell as reward or punishment *after* death. They believed God rewarded or punished humans in *this* life. God, using the Earth, through so-called natural or man-made calamities, would punish sinfulness.

> The LORD has sworn by the pride of Jacob:
> Surely I will never forget any of their deeds.
> Shall not the land tremble on this account,
>   and everyone mourn who lives in it . . . ?
> The time is surely coming, says the Lord GOD,
>   when I will send famine on the land.
>
> (Amos 8:7-8, 11)

For the prophets, the cleansing of pollution required radical changes in us—repentance—and they called upon their leaders and the people to confess their transgressions. They called upon all to reestablish just, respectful relationships with God, with society, and, not least, with nature:

> Therefore hear the words of the LORD, you scoffers
>   who rule this people in Jerusalem.
> Because you have said, "We have made a covenant
>   with death . . .
> when the overwhelming scourge passes through
>   it will not come to us;
> for we have made lies our refuge,
>   and in falsehood we have taken shelter";
>   therefore thus says the Lord GOD, . . .
> I will make justice the line,
>   and righteousness the plummet . . .
> Then your covenant with death will be annulled . . .
> Now therefore do not scoff,
>   or your bonds will be made stronger;
>   for I have heard a decree of destruction
>   from the Lord GOD of hosts upon the whole land.
> Listen, and hear my voice;
>   Pay attention, and hear my speech.
>
> (Isaiah 28:14-18, 22-23)

Without repentance we cannot establish the one, firm basis for the proper relationship to nature. The prophetic approach to pollution is thus radical—going to the root—rather than technical, adjusting the details.

Today those who strive to protect the environment trace many connections between social injustice and environmental degradation. It has been said that the poor harm the Earth out of need and the rich out of greed. The impact of human culture upon the biosphere is now profound. We may be sure there are many more connections between human sinfulness and environmental destruction that we have not yet analyzed, and some that we may never know. A relationship to the living world based on moral principles and faith in a Creator God remains our best protection.

Truly, O people in Zion, inhabitants of Jerusalem, you shall weep no more. He will surely be gracious to you at the sound of your cry; when he hears it, he will answer you. Though the Lord may give you the bread of adversity and the water of affliction, yet your Teacher will not hide . . . any more, but your eyes shall see your Teacher. And when you turn to the right or when you turn to the left, your ears shall hear a word behind you, saying, "This is the way; walk in it . . ."

He will give rain for the seed with which you sow the ground, and grain, the produce of the ground, which will be rich and plenteous. On that day your cattle will graze in broad pastures; and the oxen and donkeys that till the ground will eat silage, which has been winnowed with shovel and fork. On every lofty mountain and every high hill there will be brooks running with water . . . on the day when the LORD binds up the injuries of his people, and heals the wounds inflicted by his blow (Isaiah 30:19-21, 23-26).

THE KINGDOM OF GOD: JESUS' EMBRACE OF THIS WORLD

"In the beginning was the Word" (John 1:1).

Opening his gospel with a meditation on the Word of God, John identified Christ with the whole creative process:

In the beginning was the Word,
and the Word was with God,
and the Word was God.
He was in the beginning with God.
All things came into being through him,
and without him, not one thing came into being.
What has come into being in him was life,
and the life was the light of all people.
The light shines in the darkness,
and the darkness did not overcome it (John 1:1-5).

Out of this creative process emerged the world.

The phrase "without him, not one thing came into being" shows that John associated Christ with the creation of all things, including all species. Often, the popular concept of the Christian tradition ignores this most important aspect of the reality of Jesus. Many Christians focus only on the redemptive role of Jesus for human beings; they fail to recognize the prior importance of his creative role in the unfolding drama of creation or the place all creation has in redemption.

Jesus came to this Earth to renew *his* creation. Jesus came with saving love not only to the human species, but to the *whole* of creation. New Testament authors recognized that Jesus' saving act was a creative act that revitalized nature as well as the human spirit.

Luke records that Jesus' concern for the creatures of the Earth went far beyond the value that human commerce placed on them: "Are not five sparrows sold for two pennies? Yet not one of them is forgotten in God's sight" (Luke 12:6). Paul, convinced that the new covenant was coming alive in Christian life, remembered nature's interest in liberation: "For the creation waits with eager longing for the revealing of the children of God ... in hope that the creation itself will be set free from its bondage to decay and will obtain the freedom of the glory of the children of God" (Romans 8:19-21).

The kingdom that Jesus announced embraced the life of this world—animal, vegetable, and human. John in his gospel said that God gave Jesus to our world because God "so loved the world" (John 3:16). The closeness of Jesus to the natural world and his love for it are ever before us in the scriptures. It is especially clear in the sermons he gave and the stories he told to bring home the deep lessons of life, stories of the birds of the air, the wild flowers in the field, the grain of wheat.

In preparation for his ministry Jesus spent time in the wilderness. There he allowed himself to be tempted by enticements to which many have fallen victim. When he was hungry, he was tempted perhaps to force the earth to produce more food than it could in its natural rhythms. Today, in many nations, humans use petrochemical fertilizers and irrigation to force the soil to produce crops far beyond its natural capacities. In the dereliction of his solitude, he most certainly resisted the temptation to exercise the power of an earthly ruler. Today we continue to war over power. Weary and discouraged, he may have been tempted to throw himself from the top of the temple pinnacle (Matthew 4:1-11). Today many, having lost their sense of respect for life, give in to the temptation to seek release in drugs, alcohol, and suicide. Such temptations invite humans to look at creation as a means of satisfying human needs and desires. Jesus endured these temptations so that we might learn to reject them.

Jesus condemned the greed for power and wealth, which brings about unnecessary poverty and inhuman oppression. He used the example of a farmer whose land gave a rich harvest:

"The land of a rich man produced abundantly. And he thought to himself, 'What should I do, for I have no place to store my crops?' Then he said, 'I will do this: I will pull down my barns and build larger ones, and there I will store all my grains and my goods. And I will say to my soul: "Soul, you have ample goods laid up for many years; relax, eat, drink, be merry."' But God said to him, 'You fool! This very night your life is being demanded of you. And the things you have prepared, whose will they be?'" (Luke 12:16-20).

For Jesus, it was wrong to store up excess produce selfishly and keep it from the poor, the hungry, and even the wild animals. For Jesus, thankfulness for the gift of Earth's bounty and a proper relation with God mattered far more than building new storehouses.

To reemphasize the foolishness of the ways of the human species Jesus alluded to a wild flower: "Do not worry about your life . . . Consider the lilies, how they grow: they neither toil nor spin; yet I tell you, even Solomon in all his glory was not clothed like one of these" (Luke 12:22, 27).

In a later passage from the same gospel narrative, Jesus encourages us to look into nature to see the "signs of the times":

"When you see a cloud rising in the west, you immediately say, 'It is going to rain'; and so it happens. And when you see the south wind blowing, you say, 'There will be scorching heat'; and it happens" (Luke 12:54-55).

Jesus ended this teaching with a stern reprimand both for those present and for people of all times who fail to heed what is just and right in and for creation:

"You hypocrites! You know how to interpret the appearance of the earth and sky, but why do you not know how to interpret the present time? And why do you not judge for yourselves what is right?" (Luke 12:56-57).

Jesus' life work continued the creative process, teaching humans to become creative. Jesus, indeed, came to bring salvation to all, and to humankind he entrusted the fate of the cosmos.

Not everyone was or is willing to listen to this message of salvation and repentance. Jesus carried on his mission in the face of strong opposition. They called him a fool, a traitor, a blasphemer! Jesus endured humiliation and death to renew the lives of others and of the Earth. His love, the divine love of the Word made flesh, is consistently self-giving.

We, like Jesus before us, are called to bring a saving love to this creation and to acknowledge the wrong that we have done to God's creation. The survival of all depends on our commitment to a loving and life-giving communion with creation.

CHRISTIAN COMMUNITY AND THE EARTH

Our times call for us to reinterpret our relation to God's beautiful creation, the Earth, the universe. Christians are called to form a community that embraces God's creation and maintains fellowship with our companions of all species. This calling requires us to open our hearts to the Earth — to see, hear, taste, smell, and feel — so we may come to experience the communion of creation.

We do well to remind ourselves of Paul's sermon to the people in Lystra, who believed Paul and Barnabas to be Greek gods (Zeus and Hermes), because they had healed a crippled man. Paul and Barnabas tell the people they are not gods, because there is a

"living God, who made the heaven and the earth and the sea and all that is in them. In past generations he allowed all the nations to follow their own ways; yet he has not left himself without a witness in doing good — giving you rains from heaven and fruitful seasons, and filling you with food and your hearts with joy." Even with these words, they scarcely restrained the crowds from offering sacrifice to them (Acts 14:15-18).

Would that we could respond as passionately to these words as the crowds did!

When we open ourselves to the needs of the natural world, we will also experience pain. The closer a person is to creation, the deeper will be that person's experience of the pain that creation suffers. The joy of being alive to the beauty of nature will, however, outweigh the suffering. In order to feel pleasure we must accept our vulnerability to pain. We then learn the virtues of humility, compassion, and discernment.

Already many Christians who serve the afflicted or stand with the oppressed expose themselves to suffering that they might have avoided had they remained detached. In the tropical forests of Brazil, Francisco (Chico) Mendez, a rubber tapper, labored to preserve the forests and the way of life of his people. Chico was murdered in the fall of 1988 by a group of cattle ranchers opposed to sustainable, nonharmful use of the forest.

In John's gospel Christ is identified with all of creation and the whole creative act. Therefore, it is important for Christians to recognize Christ's spirit in nature. We must seek the crucified and risen Christ in that unfolding creative act, in the life of creation, not only in our churches. Christians may then respond with respect and care for nature, upheld by the inspiration of serving Christ.

Many hear the cry of the Lord in the passage from Matthew that tells of our ideal relationship with other human beings:

"Then the king will say . . . 'Come, you that are blessed by my Father, inherit the kingdom prepared for you from the foundation of the world, for I was hungry and you gave me food, I was thirsty, and you gave me something to drink, I was a stranger and you welcomed me, I was naked and you gave me clothing, I was sick and you took care of me, I was in prison and you visited me.' Then the righteous will answer him, 'Lord, when was it that we saw you hungry and gave you food, or thirsty and gave you something to drink? And when was it that we saw you a stranger and welcomed you, or naked and gave you clothing? And when was it that we saw you sick or in prison and visited you?' And the king will answer them, 'Truly I tell you, just as you did it to one of the least of these who are members of my family, you did it to me' " (Matthew 25:34-40).

Some see Christ hungry, thirsty, and imprisoned behind despoiled landscapes, abused animals, endangered species, and poisoned ecosystems. They see that today Christ's suffering body extends to what is eroded, polluted, endangered, or valued only for human use. The world humans are abusing in a real sense is the body of our Lord.

To take delight in nature is to join Jesus in a cosmic salvific act. Are we to stand by as God anguishes over the cry of wild birds covered with sludge? Do we remain indifferent as the Creator weeps with the dolphins into whose habitat we unthinkingly dump nuclear waste? Christ, the central point of human history and creation, mourns over this bloody despoliation.

In defacing the cosmos we deface the image of Christ, the Word. No longer can we afford to stand idly by aware of such exploitation.

Paul, whose meditations on Christ may be unsurpassed, assures us that the call to reconciliation "is from God, who reconciled us to himself through Christ, and has given us the ministry of reconciliation" (2 Corinthians 5:18). Paul saw Christ as the new Adam, the first of God's new children. We, baptized into Christ and living as Christ's ministers, must heal the wounds inflicted by human sinfulness on nature, "for the creation waits with eager longing for the revealing of the children of God" (Romans 8:19).

Those who work to redeem nature from pollution share in Christ's sufferings. This trial, however, offers special rewards. "For just as the sufferings of Christ are abundant for us," the apostle Paul writes, "so also our consolation is abundant through Christ" (2 Corinthians 1:5). We are among the children of God for whom creation holds its breath, waiting "with eager longing" (Romans 8:19).

Despair over the fate of human society and the natural world is not Christian. Our acceptance of the message of Jesus is pivotal. In order to heal a broken world, we turn to God, who creates, sustains, and redeems in Christ through the Holy Spirit. It is this trust in the Creator on which the whole law and the prophets is based. It is this trust in the loving God, the giver of life, which nourishes and focuses our hope for reconciliation and new life.

KEY SCRIPTURE REFERENCES

Hebrew Scriptures

Genesis
1
2:4b-17
9:1-17
Exodus
20:8-11
23:10-12
Leviticus
25:23
Deuteronomy
8:7-20
11:1-15
27:19-22
28:1-24
Job
12:7-15
12:38-39
38:39-41
39:1-8

Psalms
8
24:1-4
50:10-12
65:9-13
96:10-13
104
145:9,14-
16
146:5-7
147
148
Isaiah
1:16-17
10:1-2
11:1-10
24:1-13
28:14-23

30:19-26
42:5-9
45:18-19
55:12-13
58:6-10
65:17-25
Jeremiah
2:1-7
27:5-7
Ezekiel
34:17-19
Hosea
2:18-20
4:1-3
Amos
4:13
8:7-11

Christian Scriptures

Matthew
4:1-11
6:24-34
25:35-40
Luke
12
John
1:1-5
3:16-21

Romans
1:20-22
8:19-25
1 Corinthians
4:1-2
2 Corinthians
1:5
5:18

Colossians
1:15-20
1 Timothy
4:1-5
Hebrews
4:12-13
Revelation
10:5-7

SUGGESTIONS FOR INDIVIDUAL REFLECTION
OR GROUP DISCUSSION

1. Read the following litany aloud or silently. Pause for silent reflection. Then meditate on your "part" of Christ's body. Describe specifically how it contributes to or takes away from the soundness of the whole.

Leader: The planet is one and has many nations, but all are members. All of us have been given to drink of the Spirit.

Response: Now the planet has not one member, it has many. North America cannot say to Australia, Oceania, or Asia, "I do not need you."

Leader: ... any more than Africa and Europe can say to South America, "We do not need you."

Response: God so constructed the planet that all the members must be concerned for one another.

Leader: If one part is hurt, all parts are hurt with it. If one part is honored, all parts are honored.

Response: You together are Christ's body, but each of you is a different part of it.

2. Retell in your own words the biblical creation story. Then read the Earth Covenant (see Appendix 4). Decide upon concrete steps you and your community can undertake to fulfill the Earth Covenant. Create a prayer that expresses your covenant with the Creator God to protect the Earth.

3. Rewrite Psalm 104 to illustrate the natural environment that surrounds you.

4. If you consider God to be the landholder, as did the Israelites, what steps are needed to change the types of private, public, and collective land ownership with which you are familiar?

5. In what ways does a sense of justice and compassion for neighbors provide more "social security" than food stored in

barns and assets secured in banks? Elaborate on specific examples from your own life experience or from current events. What positive steps can you suggest to change the present system?

6. Read or enact "A New Decalogue" (see Appendix 3). You may read it responsively or act it out (the narrator reads "God's" voice and the rest of the group creates a drama, dance, or pictorial representation of what is read).

7. Think about these questions. How do you answer them?
   a. Do I think of Jesus' love for creation when I am impressed by a sunset, sunrise, flower, or other natural scene? Do I thank him?
   b. What can I do to help others appreciate the world around us as God's gift to us?
   c. Can I speak to God as Creator, giver of life and all good gifts to me? Do I thank God each day? Do I praise God for being so generous to me?

CHAPTER 6

Ecological Healing

A Christian Response

Christians, like people of other faiths, have entered into the ecological debate rather late, at a time when much ecological damage has been done. In the past Christians have placed much emphasis on the effect of sin on individuals rather than society. Little was said about the corporate sins of greed and materialism committed against the Earth. Little guidance was given for the building of new structures that would safeguard God's creation. The question of how our beliefs implied responsibility to act against environmental deterioration in our neighborhoods, towns, or nations did not seem urgent.

All this is changing. Many Christians and many Christian communities have joined with other peoples throughout the world in befriending and defending the Earth. Indeed, in many places Christian communities have raised a prophetic voice, sometimes in the face of government opposition and even repression. Much more needs to be done: concrete actions, development of responsive theology, discussions between Christian theologians and scientists, conversion in world-view and lifestyle, discernment, and prayer—all these will help us to "respond to the signs of the times."

MODERN THEOLOGICAL RESPONSES

A number of contemporary Christian theologians have grappled with human accountability for the fate of the Earth and how this affects Christian theology. We have chosen to present the views of three theologians so engaged. We do so in the hope that their contributions will encourage and help each of us to bring closer together problems of ecology and faith. Each theologian we discuss represents a different perspective on a common theme: faith and the environmental and social crises of our day. To begin, we briefly place each theologian within a context of theological work being done today, for each represents a particular school of thought in Christianity.

With respect to the Passionist priest Thomas Berry there is no mistaking his wonder and joy over the Earth's evolutionary history and its revelatory dimension. He stresses the great importance of human consciousness of the Earth. This approach is in line with that of the Jesuit Teilhard de Chardin and Protestants John Cobb and Jürgen Moltmann. These are process theologians, concerned with the process of divine involvement in human/Earth life.

Sallie McFague, our second theologian, holds up to us new images of God and of the Earth. She, like some other theologians such as Rosemary Radford Ruether, expresses deep concern about patriarchal images of God and their negative influence on human care of the Earth. Such theologians are concerned with restoring interconnecting areas of life that were separated during the Enlightenment (body and spirit, mind and nature, male and female, spirit and Earth, God and human).

The third representative is Loren Wilkinson, who represents the stewardship school of Christian response. This school of thought tends to focus on humans and what they should do to care for the Earth. Theologians of this school are concerned with how Jews and Christians should respond faithfully to God's statement to humankind: "Be fruitful and multiply, and fill the earth and subdue it; and have dominion over the fish of the sea and over the birds of the air and over every living thing that moves upon the earth" (Genesis 1:28).

Still other theologians working on Christian response to the Earth from a variety of perspectives include Walter Brueggemann, Richard Cartwright Austin, H. Paul Santmire, Joseph Sittler, Matthew Fox, D. J. Hall, Dieter Hessel, Mary Evelyn Jergen, Dorothee Soelle, and Roger Shinn.

THE EARTH AS REVELATORY—THOMAS BERRY

Thomas Berry is one of the most provocative figures of modern times. For many years he has been called a "prophet in the wilderness."[1] To put Berry's work in its proper context one must first grasp the gravity of the ecological crisis that our world is facing and the role that the human species has had in bringing the Earth into that crisis. The crisis has been brought about not only by our economic systems, but also by our world-views, which have fostered an understanding of humans as the supreme reality that gives value to the Earth and all other species. Such a narrow world-view restricts human thinking and restricts the life of the planet. Berry asks the troubling question, Are humans—who are absolutely dependent on the environment, which they exploit and degrade—a viable species on this planet?

Most "modern" people work within a world that can be measured, graphed, photographed, mapped, and studied in both its historical and current dimensions. But the world that Berry's vision encompasses is something more. Creation is developing. It is so filled with realities that the human cannot see what is immediately in front of the eye or hear what is crying out to the ear. The full reality of the Earth escapes the narrow range of sensitivity allowed to us by the industrial, technological world in which we live. To get back in touch with the real world—the Earth and the universe—Berry tells us that we need to rediscover the long sequence of events that have formed the human species and brought us to this point.

Berry rejoices over the Earth's evolutionary history and its revelatory dimension. As a cultural historian, Berry has made a particular study of the religious traditions of the world as well as the scientific tradition of the past few centuries. When Berry writes of the Earth, he writes from a vision influenced by his studies of modern and medieval Europe, by his encounter with the cultural traditions of India, Japan, and China, and by his study of indigenous traditions, especially those of North America. He has reflected on the biological sciences, astronomy, and physics. He has analyzed the institutions and systems of the modern world: the corporation, the economic system, the technological process, the legal tradition, the educational process.

From this store of knowledge Berry offers a challenge and a healing vision for people and for the Earth. The challenge is the recognition that the western world has substituted the myth of progress based on production and accumulation of material goods for the vision of the coming Kingdom of God on Earth. By contrast, the healing vision is founded on two realities that give meaning to all else — the Creator and the universe. When one speaks of the Creator, one speaks of a reality without comparison. Any attributes that the human mind might assign to the Creator utterly fail to describe the beginning of everything. The same is true for the reality of the universe. It can be compared to nothing known to the human experience. It has impelled the genesis and evolution of all that is for billions of years.

While Berry bases his writings on the findings of contemporary science, he pleads with contemporary scientists to go beyond the measurable realities of the Earth and universe so that they can hear and see the significance of their discoveries. Talking to physicist Brian Swimme, Berry exclaimed: "You scientists have this stupendous story of the universe. It breaks outside all previous cosmologies. But so long as you persist in understanding it solely from a quantitative mode you fail to appreciate its significance. You fail to hear its music. That's what the spiritual traditions can provide. Tell the story, but tell it with a feel for its music."[2] Thus Berry stresses the great importance of a joyful human consciousness of the Earth and sees this as basic to Christian life and to answers to our present environmental crisis.

Berry writes of an Earth that begins with the story of the origin and development of the universe as a whole. Understanding human beginnings in terms of the universe as a whole, Berry maintains, empowers us to "reinvent" the human within the unfolding drama of creation. When we are once again in communion with the universe, freed from the narrow windows of sensitivity imposed on us by industrial society and narrow world-views, we can know what we are about as a species. Getting in touch again with the Earth will reawaken in us a sense of the sacredness of the natural world, of God present to us in and through the ongoing creative process.

Berry considers today and every day, every moment, a new moment of revelation. In each moment we are made aware of how the Divine operates in and through the universe. Our degradation of the universe is then a degradation of the image of the Divine throughout the universe. If we work to enhance the Earth and the universe, to understand it in our moment, to preserve it into the future, we work to enhance and understand the image of the Divine and to preserve it into the future.

Understanding the Divine as alive in our universe, in our moment, leads us, according to Berry, to a new understanding of the Trinity. For Berry, the Trinity no longer exists in the familiar divine family (Father, Son, and Holy Spirit) but rather in a communal mode (Community, Diversity, Subjectivity). For Berry this mode of being is expressed in our universe, which, as science shows us, is a community of diverse subjects (not objects), alive and giving life to one another in our time, in our universe — God among us.

With this as his premise, Berry unfolds his vision of an *ecozoic age*, which he sees emerging in our day. This is the new era, following those geologic eras that have marked stages in the evolution of planetary life forms (Cenozoic, Mesozoic, Paleozoic, and so on). In the ecozoic age the *primacy* of the Earth will give meaning to all human action and thinking. The Earth will be recognized for what it is — the foundation for everything. The role of the human is to accept, protect, and foster the Earth's minerals, plant, and animal species — and fellow human beings — and to rejoice in the fact of the universe itself. Such a community of species, living as one through communion, expressing the image of God and the life of God among us, will, in Berry's thinking, lead to true development and true peace as creation continues in our day and into the future.

NEW MODELS OF GOD — SALLIE McFAGUE

Sallie McFague, professor of theology at Vanderbilt Divinity School, Nashville, Tennessee, inquires into what the present crises, ecological and nuclear, can help us understand about God and about ourselves. In *Models of God: Theology for an Ecological, Nuclear Age* she rejects the Enlightenment perspective, which separates God and humans, God and nature. This understanding that God was separate from the world helped Christians during that period see themselves as separate from everything else. The world was there for humans to use as they wished, with God taking a benign, distant interest. Traditional Christian pictures of God, such as a king and a father, did not change this perspective much. If God is a king, and Christians are his subjects, they can rule over other people and nature, just as God does.

Sallie McFague argues that these views are a threat today. Christians have an opportunity, she suggests, to think again about how they see God. Perhaps some of us are so used to thinking of God as a king or father that we forget these are images or metaphors only. God is *not* an autocratic king or a tyrannical father. Most of us realize in using such terms that we are saying that God *in part* and *sometimes* acts like a king or father. Are these images of God enough? Would others help us more? Why should we be asking these questions today?

McFague believes there are at least four good reasons for rethinking our views of God. First, how we view God affects how we view ourselves, our role in the world, our responsibility for the fate of the world.[3] Second, our viewpoints are critical precisely because humankind today has unprecedented power. Humans hold in their hands the fate of many millions of species, including their own. Third, we can and should reenvision God because, in looking at scripture, we realize its authority comes from its being a record of many peoples' experiences of God through the centuries. Jews and Christians in biblical times encountered a God who was present, loving, challenging, demanding, and surprising. And they responded as people always and inevitably do, from within their context and situation. Just so, we encounter the living God in our unique situation and respond as the people we are in the late twentieth century. Finally, like God, Jesus was a destabilizing, upsetting, loving presence. He challenged people to look beyond their personal limitations, their cultural confines, their social status, and their current religious beliefs. He offered a new metaphor for God: "When you pray, say 'Abba.' " Therefore, Christians today should look for a God who destabilizes, loves, is present, is unhierarchical, and who challenges us in our faith and social context.

What then, says McFague, might be the metaphors that present such a destabilizing, challenging, loving God to us today? She suggests two: the Earth should be seen as God's body; and God acting in the world should be seen as a mother, lover, and friend (a kind of new Trinity). Let us look at each of these images briefly.

To say that the Earth is God's body implies God's deep involvement, consciousness, awareness, and empathy with the Earth. God responds to the Earth just as we respond to our bodies. Our bodies are part of us, but we are not only our bodies. "The earth is charged with the grandeur of God," Gerard Manley Hopkins tells us. God is deeply sympathetic and responsive to the Earth. God suffers when any part of the Earth suffers; God rejoices when any part of the universe experiences ecstasy and fulfillment.

The Earth as God's body may seem a strange concept to some. Yet, John's gospel states that God so loved the world that God sent the Son. Is not this deep, passionate love and bonding with the Earth? The gospel did not say that God came only for human beings. Further, we now know that humans, if they live a meaningful, healthy life, are deeply connected with other people and their environment. Why should God not be so connected?

To see the Earth as God's body would, for Christians, profoundly change our relationship to it. We, if we love God, would suffer the loss of a marsh or a bird species, the suffering of women, men, and children in a famine, as rents in the fabric of the whole body of life we share with God. An injury to the world would be an injury to ourselves and our Maker.

Now, let us turn to the image of God as mother. This too may seem a startling image. Yet for thousands of years Jews and Christians have spoken of God as father, knowing all the while that God is more than a mother or a father. What we have been saying is that God's love is like a parent's love.

How is God like a mother? Asking this question helps us reaffirm qualities of God's love that may be lost to us if we only say God is fatherly. God creates, gives birth to, nurtures the world. God loves the world as both mothers and fathers love children. God consistently and watchfully cares for the fulfillment and creative life of offspring. God, as parent, loves life. God cares not only about the life of one species, the human, but a variety of life forms, interrelated in complex ways beyond our knowing or imagining and each fostering the other. God also cares for future life, for future generations. In doing so, God cares passionately for justice. Justice means the proper ordering of the world so that life, in its rich complexity and intermingling, may flourish. God's love is passionate, but a love, like a good mother's love, that nurtures the child into freedom and strength. To see God as mothering the Earth would encourage us to become like God, a universal parent.

How would seeing God as a lover help us value the world, so necessary in this time of crisis? As a lover values the beloved, God values the world. God is not so much continually attempting to save a fallen creation, as some traditional theology suggests, but rather, God loves an intrinsically valuable universe. (McFague asks whether it isn't better to be loved because we are valuable than to be loved despite our failings. This is the best of human love. Why cannot God participate in that kind of love?) God as lover needs and desires the world. God lovingly wants the creation to be whole and in balance. In this view sin is disordered love of self, refusing to see the interconnectedness of ourselves, the world, and God. Salvation is the restoration of harmony. Salvation is continual, not a once-and-for-all historical act in Christ's death and resurrection. Salvation becomes the illumination that we and all creation are deeply and passionately valued by God. This awareness alone gives us courage to participate with God in willing the Earth's wholeness and in acting for it. In acting to care for the world and its peoples and creatures, we participate in our own salvation and are healed ourselves. This view of salvation keeps us from thinking that a technical "fix" for the world's problems is enough. Salvation is not a cure but a process of working and being with God, restoring creation to wholeness.

Finally, in McFague's view, how does the metaphor of God as friend help us? The qualities of friendship, such as attraction, joy, freedom, trust, sharing a common vision, are felt by Christians for a God lovingly involved in this world. God as friend is steadfastly committed to this world, to its redemption and healing.

> It is, above all, our willingness to grow up and take responsibility for the world that the model of friend underscores. If God is the friend of the world, the one committed to it, who can be trusted never to betray it, who not only likes the world but has a vision for its well-being, then we as the special part of the body—the *imago dei*—are invited as friends of the Friend of the world to join in that vision and work for its fulfillment. God as lover of the world gave us the vision that God finds the world valuable and desires its wounds healed and its creatures free; God as friend asks us, as adults, to become associates in that work. The right name for those involved in this ongoing, sustaining, trustworthy, committed work for the world is neither parents nor lovers but friends.[4]

To see ourselves united with God and others in care for this world affirms a bond of inclusiveness. It denies credibility to those who see the world as forever divided into hostile groups, using violence to further their ends. To see God as friend committed on our and the world's behalf "defies despair." "When we pray for our friend the Earth, for whose future we fear, we hand it over not to the enemy but to the Friend who is freely, joyfully, and permanently bonded to this, our beloved world."[5] We find courage to act.

McFague states that all wondering about God is just that; we might even call these metaphors for God nonsense. But some nonsense is better than others. What images of God help us to love and care for this world? McFague entices Christians to respond.

HUMANS AS STEWARDS OF THE EARTH—LOREN WILKINSON

Loren Wilkinson's *Earthkeeping: Christian Stewardship of Natural Resources* focuses on how humans should become stewards of the Earth. Let us trace his argument.

To understand what humans should do, Wilkinson confronts head-on the question, Where is God? Because God's separation from nature is often considered responsible for the problem, should God be considered apart from nature, or one with nature? Wilkinson's answer is twofold. First, the Creator God in Genesis is separate from and transcendent from nature. God is not part of creation. But God affirms creation as good. However, the Christian God is not only transcendent but incarnate, immanent, through Christ. So, God is both apart from and within creation.

The same may be said of human beings. They are apart from nature. In the Garden of Eden story, Wilkinson reminds us, Adam has the responsibility for naming all the creatures. Adam and Eve are thus superior to the creatures, knowing them empathetically and concretely (naming in the Hebrew context means knowledge of something in its essence). But they are also creatures, sharing creaturely existence in all its aspects. So humans, like God but much more so, are a part of nature. Wilkinson calls humans "soulish dust."[6] He then ponders: What is unique about human beings? What makes humans different from other creatures? Before recent research on animal behavior told us otherwise, many believed that humans alone made tools, used reason, and thought in symbols. Now we know none of these is unique to us. Wilkinson says that the human uniqueness is our accountability to God, expressed in the Garden of Eden story. We, in Adam and Eve, were given the task of taking care of the Garden. Our vocation as humans is to be caretakers of creation. To be fully human is to steward: "Accountability to God and embeddedness in nature make the human perfectly constituted to carry out the task of stewardship."[7] Now, what is it to be a steward? We have before us the example of Christ:

> who, though he was in the form of God,
>   did not regard equality with God
>   as something to be exploited,
> but emptied himself,
>   taking the form of a slave,
>   being born in human likeness (Philippians 2:6-7).

To be a steward is to be a servant. In order to truly be a servant, we need to know the qualities and needs of the creatures over which we exercise stewardship, or for whom we are servants. We must all study ecology in order to do this. We also must gain the wisdom to ponder and balance the needs of human beings, including future generations, in case by case decisions, with the needs of other species. Human beings, for Wilkinson, are more important than fish or chickens. Yet certain goals, such as mining in an area that is home to an endangered plant, should be challenged. To be stewards also requires an understanding of justice, of just distribution of the world's resources, so that at a minimum all human beings have their basic needs met and are in a position to exercise the rights and perils of stewardship.

The Christian steward adopts in all decision making Aldo Leopold's dictum:

A thing is right when it tends to preserve the integrity, stability, and beauty of the biotic community. It is wrong when it tends otherwise.[8]

Each of us can exercise stewardship, but we must be aware that it is a shared, collective responsibility. Each of us individually exercises varied degrees of power. We are all part of larger systems. Therefore we make individual personal choices for caretaking. But we also pressure groups and systems to bring about change. The final goal is reestablishment of harmony between God and creation, and between human beings and the Earth.

Wilkinson formulates an action plan for humans as stewards. He argues:

The exercise of power inherent in our dominion must be rooted in knowledge, wisdom, and wonder . . .

We have the responsibility to provide for future generations at least the same opportunities for resource use that we inherited from earlier generations. And we should not impose on future generations any responsibilities greater than those which prior generations have left for us . . .

The time horizon for our long-term planning must be very broad, [and] . . . in exploring alternatives to our present pattern of resource use, we must be sure that we reckon properly with all of the costs involved . . .

Since it is clear that we must rapidly shift from use of "savings" resources (fossil fuels) to use of "income" resources, we should give our greatest attention to the development and widespread use of solar energy conversion devices . . .

Our aid to developing nations should work to encourage and enhance the cultural uniqueness of the nation and not to impose Western ideas on it . . .

We should remove trade practices which prevent self-development, and encourage countries to process their own raw materials . . .

We should cease activities which increase destructive urbanization.[9]

Common themes are quite discernable in the theologies of Thomas Berry, Sallie McFague, and Loren Wilkinson. First, we need to feel again awe, wonder, and empathy for the Earth, all leading to wisdom. Second, we need to regain a sense of inter-connectedness with other peoples and the Earth. Third, we must challenge and critique the basic structures and institutions, as well as philosophical underpinnings, of our societies in light of the first two principles. The created world can no longer be considered as of benefit only to humans. It has intrinsic value. We must challenge the basic economic system, of which most nations around the world are a part, which tells us otherwise.

MAJOR CHURCH STATEMENTS

Around the world the Roman Catholic Church and Protestant denominations, as well as ecumenical groups, have exhorted Christians to feel the plight of the Earth and the poor and to take action. As we began writing this book, many people sent us such statements. Some are included here. They provide information, convey grief and contrition, express compassion, and take a prophetic stance. They summon believers to a similar posture.

THE ROMAN CATHOLIC RESPONSE

The Catholic Bishops' Conference of the Philippines decried the desperate situation in its country in the widely read and lovingly evocative Pastoral Letter entitled simply, *What Is Happening To Our Beautiful Land?*

One does not need to be an expert to see what is happening and to be profoundly troubled by it. Within a few short years brown, eroded hills have replaced luxuriant forests in many parts of the country. We see dried up river beds where, not so long ago, streams flowed throughout the year . . .

As we reflect on what is happening in the light of the Gospel we are convinced that this assault on Creation is sinful and contrary to the teachings of our faith . . .

We are not alone in our concern. Tribal people all over the Philippines, who have seen the destruction of their world at close range, have cried out in anguish . . .

We often use the word progress to describe what has taken place over the past few decades. But can we say that there is real progress? . . . God, who created this beautiful land, will hold us responsible for plundering it and leaving it desolate. So will future generations of Filipinos . . .

Despite the pain and despoliation which we have mentioned, there are signs of hope. Our forefathers and our tribal brothers and sisters today still attempt to live in harmony with nature. They see the Divine Spirit in the living world and show their respect through prayers and offerings . . .

As Christians we also draw our vision from Christ . . . Our faith tells us that Christ is the center point of human history and Creation . . . The destruction of any part of Creation, especially the extinction of species, defaces the image of Christ.[10]

The Catholic bishops of the Dominican Republic recognized the urgency of the situation in their country and addressed the people prophetically on the eve of the installation of a new government in August of 1982:

We can no longer fail to concern ourselves with the preservation and betterment of the environment in which we live. No ecological imbalance comes about by itself. The sin of humanity against nature always has its repercussions against humanity. The destruction of our forests, without an effective re-forestation effort, is already bringing with it dire consequences for our rivers, our lands and our climate. It is urgent, then, that there be a well-planned and demanding policy concerning this national problem.[11]

Five years later the same bishops felt compelled to write a further Pastoral Letter on the same subject.

There has been a consensus on . . . points that we would like to emphasize:
— Ecological problems, instead of getting better, have worsened.
— The determining factor in this situation is the impunity with which offenders have worked against nature.
— Another serious factor is the situation of poverty of many Dominicans which all but forces them to destroy nature . . .
God in . . . wisdom and power created — brought into existence out of nothing that previously existed — the universe, and within that universe the planet earth, according to the marvelous laws . . . bestowed on this universe . . .
Therefore, to use human intelligence and skills (science and technology) to destroy or to threaten the earth, or not to use them when difficulties or new and varied challenges arise, is a contradiction, an abuse of the divine plan and an affront to the will of the Creator who is absolute Lord of the earth and of humankind . . .
In the case of non-renewable resources, the highly industrialized and developed countries may not exercise a sort of monopoly on the exploitation and use of these resources, without taking into account the present and future needs of the countries that are suppliers of these resources . . .
Everything we have said will simply be like words blowing in the wind if little or nothing is done. There is a great need for effective and coordinated action . . . The measures taken, however, must be twofold: technical and ethical.[12]

In recent years Catholic bishops around the world have made similar statements. The bishops challenge Christians to respond to environmental degradation, the plight of the poor, and the need for responsible stewardship of the Earth.

On 1 January 1990 Pope John Paul II issued an environmental message. He went so far as to state:

> World peace is threatened ... by a lack of due respect for nature, by the plundering of natural resources ... A new ecological awareness is ... emerg[ing] which ... ought to be encouraged to develop into concrete programs and initiatives ... Modern society will find no solution to the ecological problem unless it takes a serious look at its lifestyle ... The ecological crisis has assumed such proportions as to be the responsibility of everyone.[13]

THE PROTESTANT AND ORTHODOX RESPONSE

To give a flavor of the Protestant and Orthodox response, three traditions are highlighted here along with the 1990 Justice, Peace, Integrity of Creation World Convocation Statement of the World Council of Churches. These statements emphasize God the Creator, who desires *shalom* or justice for all of creation and an interconnectedness of human concerns with the created order. The need for repentance and restraint on the part of humans, particularly those in wealthier countries, is a strong second emphasis.

The so-called peace churches have been active in the issues of food, poverty, and justice for decades. Although a particular statement on the issue is not quoted here, the Religious Society of Friends (Quakers) distinguishes itself in promoting awareness and action in these areas. The related concern of the U.S. Mennonite Central Committee is expressed in "Resolution on the World Food Crisis Reaffirmed." Adopted on 28 January 1984 it expresses deep concern for the hungry, places their plight in relation to environmental and social factors, and calls Mennonite missions and churches—and the United States government and its people—to account.

At its January 1974 annual meeting, Mennonite Central Committee ... resolved to give priority to the world food crisis in our programming for the next decade by broadening and strengthening rural development and family planning programs in developing countries ... encourag[ing] each Mennonite and Brethren in Christ household to examine its lifestyle, particularly expenditures for food ... Calling for much greater financial and material resources for development during the next five to 10 years ... Expanding our efforts to acquaint the churches of our constituency with the relationship between overconsumption on the part of North Americans and its effect upon needy people in developing countries ...

We pledge to increase the commitment and efforts we embarked upon 10 years ago ... We will (a) emphasize how the food crisis is impacted by the public policies of our governments in Canada and the United States, notably trade and international financial agreements ... (b) Implore our governments to reverse the arms race ... (c) Encourage a growing vision for sharing our material wealth in order to provide emergency food aid and support for expanding agricultural and community development programs, especially in Africa. (d) Expand our efforts toward projects and advocacy for the very poor. This will include research and extension programs emphasizing increased food production, more employment opportunities, population stabilization, and appropriate technology. (e) Develop ways to better correlate North American agriculture with problems of hunger and justice.

The Church of the Brethren in July 1990 adopted a statement "Creation Called to Care." It sounds a warning and a challenge to Christians.

Planet Earth is in danger. The accelerating ecological crisis that threatens the survival of life on earth is evident now not only to professional biologists, botanists, environmental scientists, but to all. Awareness grows that humanity is facing a global crisis. We are living in a period when what we hope for is survival . . .

The Creator-Redeemer seeks the renewal of the creation and calls the people of God to participate in saving acts of renewal. We are called to cooperate with God in the transformation of a world that has not fulfilled its divinely given potential for beauty, peace, health, harmony, justice and joy (Isa. 11:6-9, Micah 4:3-4, Eph. 2:10, Rev. 21:1-5). Our task is nothing less than to join God in preserving, renewing and fulfilling the creation. It is to relate to nature in ways that sustain life on the planet, provide for the essential material and physical needs of all humankind, and increase justice and well-being for all life in a peaceful world.

The United Church of Christ has made the integrity of creation, justice and peace (ICJP) a denominational priority. The statement "Redeeming Creation: Relating Redemption Theology and Creation Theology" wrestles with conflicts some theologians feel when they take seriously the environmental crisis. Of particular note is the tension between so-called environmentalists and peace-and-justice advocates. The first group believes that the peace-and-justice advocates ignore the biological realities on which all life, and economic and social justice, depends. The peace-and-justice advocates believe the environmentalists ignore the real suffering of people in favor of plants and animals. The UCC statement also grapples with another topic of debate: creation as opposed to redemption theology. The UCC statement has words for both the environmentalists and the peace-and-justice advocates.

No Christian theology is complete relative to biblical revelation unless it includes both creation and redemption themes. Both are present throughout the unfolding of the biblical message . . . When traditional redemption theology is held in tension with creation theology, we can see that much more is redeemed than an isolated soul. We move from a "thin" redemption toward an "abundant" redemption; each of us is connected to each other and to the created order ... The polarity most helpful in holding together creation and redemption theology is *appreciation* and *action* ...

Those who start from a theology of redemption and are sensitive to the oppression of others need to attend to the opportunities for life amid oppression, including appreciating sunsets and trees and the natural order. Those who start from a theology of creation, who appreciate sunsets and trees, need to realize that their joy cannot be full unless they reach out to those who suffer from oppression.

The Presbyterian Church in June 1990 issued a statement "Restoring Creation for Ecology and Justice: A Report of the 202nd General Assembly of the Presbyterian Church (U.S.A.)." It begins:

Creation cries out in this time of ecological crisis. Abuse of nature and injustice to people place the future in grave jeopardy. Population triples in this century. Biological systems suffer diminished capacity to renew themselves. Finite minerals are mined and pumped as if inexhaustible. Peasants are forced onto marginal lands, the soil erodes. The rich-poor gap grows wider. Wastes and poisons exceed nature's capacity to absorb them. Greenhouse gases pose the threat of global warming. Therefore God calls the Presbyterian Church (U.S.A.) to respond to the cry of creation, human and nonhuman; engage in the effort to make the 1990s the "turnaround decade," not only for reasons of prudence or survival, but because the endangered planet is God's creation; and draw upon all the resources of biblical faith and the Reformed tradition for empowerment and guidance in this adventure.

The momentum that generated the Justice, Peace, Integrity of Creation World Convocation Statement of the World Council of Churches is presented clearly in the words of the final document of that title:

> The JPIC World Convocation was intended to be a *stage in a process* called for by the Vancouver WCC Assembly (1983): for churches "to engage . . . in a conciliar process of mutual commitment (covenant) to justice, peace, and the integrity of creation." As the WCC Central Committee of 1987 said, it would be "a decisive step toward fulfilling the mandate of the Sixth Assembly . . . and mark an important stage toward common binding pronouncements and actions on the urgent question of the survival of humankind."

Before the convocation opened, meetings to consider the JPIC were held around the world, and pronouncements were issued pertinent to the host countries. The convocation met in Seoul, Korea, in March 1990.

The final document includes the following affirmation:

> Now is the time to commit ourselves to God's covenant. The moment of history is unique. All life on Earth is threatened by injustice, war and destruction of creation because we have turned away from God's covenant. Knowing of the opportunities that are offered to us, we ask for God's forgiveness.

A related vision statement sounds the themes of interconnection between humans and other species on Earth and of the need for action:

> Now is the time for the ecumenical movement to articulate its vision of all people living on earth and caring for creation as a family where each member has the same right to wholeness of life. While this vision is spiritual in nature, it must be expressed in concrete action. On the basis of our spiritual experience here in Seoul we have committed ourselves to work for:

—a just economic order and for liberation from the bondage of the foreign debt;

—the true security of all nations and people and for a culture of non-violence;

—preserving the gift of the earth's atmosphere, and for building a culture that can live in harmony with creation's integrity;

—the eradication of racism and discrimination on all levels for all people, and for the dismantling of patterns of behavior that perpetuate the sin of racism.

The Greek Orthodox Archdiocese of North and South America has published "Orthodoxy and the Ecological Crisis." This statement includes the 1989 pastoral message of the Ecumenical Patriarch. This eloquent message declares that

in the face of [the environmental crisis], the Orthodox Church cannot remain silent . . . Humanity must safeguard creation in a spirit of love and offer it in thanksgiving to the Creator . . . We paternally exhort all believers . . . to counsel themselves and their children to love, respect and protect the environment . . . [and] call on all governments to proceed without delay in every necessary action to protect and preserve the natural world which God created in all its beauty.

CONCLUSION

Orthodox, Protestant, and Roman Catholic church bodies around the world are beginning to envision a life lived by faithful people in harmony with creation. We all are called by the God whom we worship to be faithful in our love of creation and to be part of that effort.

SUGGESTIONS FOR INDIVIDUAL REFLECTION
OR GROUP DISCUSSION

1. Reflect on the views of the three theologians (Berry, McFague, Wilkinson) discussed in this chapter. With which do you agree or disagree? Why? Write your own theology of creation.

2. Describe a time when you felt close to God in nature. Draw a picture of that experience. What does it communicate to you about yourself, Christ, the Holy Spirit, God, and the world?

3. Suggest ways in which you could change your personal life or your worship life to reflect your reverence for the Earth.

4. Reread the church denominational statements. Use them to encourage reflection and actions that support sustainable use and management of local natural resources by your church and civic community.

5. What is your denomination doing to respond to the environmental crisis? How can you become more involved?

CHAPTER 7

Ecological Healing

Toward a Sustainable World

How can we heal the societies in which we live and the natural world? We do well to recall that "healing occupies a singular and prominent place in religious experience throughout the world."[1] Jesus heals as a sign that he is the Messiah, ushering in the Kingdom of God.

As we grow as Christians, we more clearly discern a call to heal. Healing is based in reverence for the Creator and the creation and calls forth appropriate concrete actions. We cannot heal the Earth without understanding it and without bringing together fragmented dimensions of life. These fragmented dimensions include the whole of life—biology and economics, religion, development, politics, and traditional and contemporary science. This approach, which embraces so many disparate studies, makes many demands on us. For many of us, thinking about economics or ecology, for example, as part of our life of faith appears disconcertingly new. But as we progress in this work, we will heal centuries-old splits that have affected our lives. What a challenge! We steer again by the stars and not by the lights of each passing ship. There is a firm biblical base to leave from and return to.

SOLUTIONS

To heal, we need a detailed diagnosis and very specific remedies. Healing remedies are based on strategies elaborated by people aware of the remaining complexities and yet who have made some progress. In order to act as healers, we need some awareness of these strategies. We group them here under the divisions of understanding, financing, and developing sustainably. A number of these proposals may seem utopian, and indeed some may well be. But history has a disconcerting way of making yesterday's utopia today's partial reality. It is in this spirit that these proposals are made.

UNDERSTANDING

Healers need understanding of the interconnections between the human species and the rest of creation. This understanding is available to us through science and indigenous knowledge.

Christians need to support scientific research about the Earth. Thomas Berry has called science one of the most extensive meditations ever on the Earth. It was a satellite that gave us the first picture in existence of our home, the Earth. Satellites give us clear pictures of forests burning and ocean pollution. Computer models are used extensively to help us anticipate global warming. Scientists are also pressing ahead in understanding the wisdom of indigenous peoples and their rich environments. To recognize and amplify indigenous knowledge, such as the use of herbal medicine, in order to benefit both traditional peoples and larger groups appears beneficial.

With urbanization and environmental destruction, many of us know less about the natural areas around us than did past generations. We benefit from learning about our environment, either close at hand or from elders who remember a richer natural landscape. Growing awareness can lead us to action to protect or restore our environment.

FINANCING

A reverence for creation oddly enough has much to do with economics. A second strategy for healing the crisis we face is to bring the Earth's ecosystem more fully into the monetary system.

We saw in Chapter 4 that modern economic systems developed out of the Age of Reason. They were based on the assumption that nature has no value in itself; thus modern societies tend to put value only on what can be bought and sold. Natural resources are not valued. If we were to place a monetary value on such scarce resources as clean air, clean water, and abundant supply of necessary foodstuffs, would this help societies to value such resources and to build economic systems that reflect such value? Some would answer yes.

Unfortunately, we cannot value natural resources financially without a struggle because there are many unknowns. How will people want to use the resources in the future? How many untapped resources are there? Further, does nature have intrinsic value, beyond whatever use humans wish to make of it? These questions have only limited answers. The marketplace, however, determines the answers without debate and usually based only on the value of immediate human demand. We could feel hopeless about valuing resources. Yet to struggle to do so links two spheres which in the Western world have been unfortunately separated, economics and ecology. To struggle to bring these two areas together may enable us to be faithful to a call as Christians to care for our home, the Earth. Otherwise the present economic system that renders nature valueless will without rebuttal answer all these questions so as to harm the environment and increase the numbers and suffering of the poor.

Clearly, the present economic system with its improper valuation of Earth's resources puts in jeopardy not only the Earth but also all future human generations. To foster an economic system that uses everything now and leaves nothing for future generations represents a cynical, materialistic, and hopeless attitude, hidden zealously under the ideal of growth. This is an attitude that has not been adopted by the many generations of humans who have gone before us.[2] It is an attitude that is in profound contrast to the religious values of many peoples, both past and present.

We need to rethink the concept of economic growth. We know that in order to grow the present economic system degrades the world's priceless natural resources, the Earth's "capital" (oil reserves, for example, built up over billions of years), to pay for present production and consumption. Yet the Earth's resources do not grow. An economic system based on unlimited growth and overuse of the Earth's capital is not compatible with an Earth of immeasurable value that evolves but does not grow. The economist Herman Daly puts it this way:

> Politically, it is difficult to admit that growth, with its almost religious connotations of ultimate goodness, must be limited. But it is precisely the non-sustainability of growth that gives urgency to the concept of sustainable development. The earth will not tolerate the doubling of even one grain of wheat sixty-four times, yet in the past two centuries we have developed a culture dependent on exponential growth for its economic stability.[3]

The principle of valuation of Earth resources should acknowledge differences between industrialized and developing nations, and emphasize ways they can help each other. The greatest amount of biodiversity exists in developing countries, in coastal mangrove areas, rain forests, and coral reefs. Developing countries can ill afford the cost of protection of such resources. Industrially developed countries, therefore, must try to value the importance of biological diversity to their own countries and their people, both present and future generations. The developed world, which benefits from biological diversity, should pay developing countries to protect and preserve their biologically rich ecosystems. Schemes for environmentally sound tourism could be part of this plan.

Various proposals — all controversial — to renegotiate third-world debt should be analyzed and carefully implemented to foster this mutual cooperation. Some argue that the official foreign debt should be canceled and the commercial debt reduced "via mechanisms equivalent to corporate bankruptcy law."[4] Others believe that the debt of developing countries needs to be renegotiated in a way that can encourage the poorer countries to safeguard their environment and enable their poor to move out of poverty. Debt interest payments could be used for development in debtor countries, with social and environmental indicators used to measure progress. However, "economic and environmental conditions imposed on debtor countries should be replaced by symmetric commitments for sustainable development in developed and developing countries alike."[5] Private debt could be bought at a discount by a newly created management authority. It would then "forgive it selectively and gradually over five to ten years to reward performance on specific environmental as well as macroeconomic policy commitments."[6]

Debt-for-nature swaps have also been implemented. They should not be negotiated without wide public debate, respect for national sovereignty and for rights of indigenous groups, and careful analysis of the social, environmental, and economic impact on the debtor countries.[7]

Developed countries can also help third-world countries diversify their economies. Substantial help by the developed world would occur through lowering the U.S. national debt, which raises interest rates worldwide, and by the developed world putting its own environmental house in order. Research monies spent on sustainable energy and agriculture in the developed world produce information that can be transmitted to planners and governments in developing countries for use in turning around their countries' unsustainable economic paths. Overall, the developed world's insistence on producing goods for affluent appetites must be altered to ensure a sustainable future.

Can we calculate the wealth (or declining wealth) of nations differently from the growth model? One suggestion is that we use an Index of Sustainable Economic Welfare (ISEW) to replace the Gross National Product (GNP).[8] The GNP, which measures only market activity, can show that a nation has increased in wealth even though its environment has deteriorated and poverty has deepened. By contrast, using the ISEW, many areas usually left out of the GNP are tabulated as costs or benefits. Some areas accounted for as either adding to a nation's wealth or subtracting from it are distributional equality, defense expenditures, expenditures on national advertising, costs of commuting, urbanization, water, air, and noise pollution, loss of wetlands and farmlands, and long-term environmental damage. Life expectancy, infant mortality, working conditions, energy efficiency ratios, and human rights and democratic participation, including the free flow of information, would also be good additional indicators.[9] More accurately measuring its wealth could help a country set new goals.

Other kinds of financing schemes would help. A carbon tax ought to be levied on fossil fuels. This tax could generate money to pay for pollution clean-up equipment, research into nonfossil fuels or nonpolluting energy sources, or incentives to companies to develop and make sustainable technology widely available. Some countries need to use taxes or subsidies applied to people or companies. (Pollution taxes would not, by themselves, stop the pollution of our environment. The cost of the tax would likely be passed on to the consumer and computed as a cost of production. Those companies that do not comply with environmental regulations and that are found to be repeated offenders should be shut down by the government and not licensed to do business in the future.) If environmental taxes weigh unfairly on the poor, the tax revenues could be recycled to offset such uneven distribution.

Another method of controlling pollution is for governments to join together to set a "per capita" quota standard for emissions of gasses that destroy the ozone layer or that add carbon dioxide in the Earth's atmosphere. Countries that exceed their "per capita" quota would be penalized until they bring emissions into compliance with world standards. Heavy polluters should not be allowed to purchase emission credits from those who create less pollution. The penalties that are levied could be "paid" in one of two ways. Foreign assistance by developed countries could foster the immediate transfer of nonpolluting, environmentally benign technologies to developing countries. Or trust funds could be set up to further scientific research into the production of nonpolluting energy sources, industrial production, and disposal processes. Centers involved in research and training for sustainable development and funded from this source could be attached to existing universities.

Further, world governing bodies or ongoing world-wide consultations could assist in identifying impediments to sustainable development. These bodies or consultations would set priorities for environmental and sustainable development activities; define legitimate trade measures to protect the environment; and help value the Earth's resources in an economic climate free of special interest demands and market pressures. Governments could support a new international ecological economics by collecting and analyzing environmental data, monitoring environmental trends, and estimating environmental costs. International and bilateral trade agreements would then be nuanced to reflect the full environmental implications of projected policies.

While pricing natural resources and properly paying for them may seem impossible, we do well to remember that the present degradation of the environment is highly inefficient, unjust, and, often, subsidized. Special interest groups, such as oil and automobile companies, pressure governments toward a favorable stance toward their market concerns. Citizens, therefore, subsidize their activities. The poor and the environment suffer terrible consequences.

DEVELOPING SUSTAINABLY

We have entered into an approach to all these issues often termed *sustainable development*. The remainder of this chapter is concerned with demonstrating what the term *sustainable development* means for human and environmental welfare.

Sustainable development has been described as a process that "seeks to develop strategies and tools to respond to five broad requirements: integration of conservation and development; satisfaction of basic human needs; achievement of equity and social justice; provision for social self-determination and cultural diversity; and maintenance of ecological integrity."[10] A sustainable economy, we have seen, cannot grow; rather, it can develop in various ways on an Earth that is evolving but limited. We may say that sustainable development enhances the indefinite thriving of both natural and social systems. It is a life so lived that the immediate needs of the Earth community are met in such a way that the web of life is nurtured into the future.

It is clear that achieving a sustainable economy will mean vast changes in the world economy. In sum, sustainable development policies and practices ensure that each and every individual has, at the very least, access to all the resources needed to meet his or her basic needs for food, shelter, health care, and education, while keeping the environment healthy. The gap between the rich and the poor will diminish. Local residents would determine how to use their natural resources and have first claim on their benefits. Only when their present needs were met and the sustainability of the resources for future generations guaranteed will excess goods be made available to other markets.

Developing sustainably demands not just a new international economic order, but creation of new attitudes, systems, and structures that respect creation and enhance people's participation at all levels in the decision-making process. "Trickle-down" and "supply-side" economic systems have little place in sustainable development. These systems thrive on outdated rugged individualism and foster materialism and, in the end, greed. Sustainable development is only possible in a climate of global cooperation that acknowledges our interdependence, promotes peace and just relationships with each other and the natural world, and sees the health of persons and the natural world as of paramount importance.

We now move to a discussion of sustainable development, touching on areas of concern within developing countries, in particular. Here we sketch in our vision of ecological healing.

THE ROLE OF WOMEN IN DEVELOPMENT

The wisdom of women, often unvoiced, should be more fully utilized by all social units — their families, communities, and governments. Barred from education and denounced for it, women are often discounted. Women need to be educated in order to assume their responsibilities.

Women have consistently been denied positions of power needed to alter the directions taken by the societies in which they live. They are often overburdened by work and undernourished. They are the world's farmers, and yet they are often poorly fed.

Many development programs affect the daily life of women, especially in rural areas. In these areas women are the gatherers of wood for cooking and water for drinking. They are gardeners, tending small plots of land on which they grow vegetables and other dietary supplements for the family. Development projects in rural areas often deal with forest regeneration, potable water supply, and backyard farming for enhanced nutrition. It is women who should plan these programs.

Women need the tools that will empower them. They want more control over their own destiny and the destiny of their families. They should not be denied access to land and the right to own and inherit land so that they and their children will have security. They need capital in order to share in the economic security of the male-dominated economies. When they enter the cultural and political arena they gain political power and have a greater say in the types of development programs their governments will seek and accept.

Along with empowerment, women should be freed from the drudgery of many daily tasks. Men must be taught and encouraged to share family responsibilities equitably.

Development agencies can assist with appropriate technologies. Appropriate water systems bring water closer to households. Fast-growing varieties of trees for firewood near to homes lessen the time women spend gathering. Bio-intensive gardens, whether in urban or rural areas, can produce a varied family diet. More appropriate and technologically advanced cooking stoves, shellers, grinders, and other labor-saving devices cut down on labor and firewood. Each of these advances may, by itself, seem rather insignificant but can make a life-saving difference to the lives of billions of women and their families.

Many women's development efforts are now thriving. In El Salvador groups of women are receiving training and credit with the purpose of forming family micro-enterprises in rural San Vicente Department. In Senegal, women whose main source of income is selling fish are learning to preserve fish and participate in a savings and loan program.

Mrs. Wangari Maathai, a former anatomy professor, has since 1977 headed the Green Belt Movement set up by the National Council of Women of Kenya. The movement helps people start green belts of at least one thousand trees. It has had the result of popularizing tree-planting movements around the world.

THE QUALITY OF HUMAN LIFE

In industrial economies today, there are many false notions about the quality of human life. The values of sound family life are often lost in the quest for material products.

Even though more and more families are sharing in higher levels of living, the costs rise in geometric proportion. In order to maintain a high standard of living in developed countries, many families need to have two or three means of income. Thus, both mother and father work and establish their individual careers. This is a very demanding, complex assignment, and it is not surprising that many fail in it. The rearing of children, in particular, becomes more and more demanding in this situation. Needless to say, in the race to accumulate material goods, many values, including time to contemplate nature, are lost.

In this realm the experience of indigenous people can serve as a warning and a model. The quality of life of the human person is not measured by things owned, but by values shared.

AGRICULTURE

Using sustainable agriculture helps us affirm that "the Earth is the Lord's and the fullness thereof." We grow crops in the soil God has given in ways that are wise and good. Through the use of sustainable agriculture, we, as one Indian development worker said, have the joy of re-creating the Garden of Eden.

Sustainable agriculture practices include intensive land use — through growing crops in rapid rotation and interplanting several crops and trees, organic farming, garden/farm agroecosystems (for fodder, fuel, and food), use of trees and shrubs to reduce desertification, and rotational grazing of stock. In the past decade urban agriculture has given people hope as urban areas — rooftops, abandoned industrial sites, roadways, military grounds — have given rise to garden produce for home and market. The use of seed diversity; allowing rice paddies to revert to their (pre-pesticide) capacity to sustain fish, frogs, and insects; and developing fish farming are also very important. The application of leaf litter and human waste as fertilizer increases soil fertility. The knowledge of indigenous farmers can be tapped for understanding of the natural environment and methods of growing or protecting a diverse variety of crops. People tending agroforestry systems can use certain plant associations and rely on natural processes — competition, predation, decomposition, and feeding — to reduce pests.

For the harsh and variable African climate and soil, *The Greening of Africa* suggests many concrete practices that lead to sustainable agriculture.[11] These include the use of legumes in intercropping as well as rotational cropping for nitrogen fixation; mulching with crop residues; and conservation of soil, water, and nutrients through building contour ridges, stone lines, trash lines, grass strips, and terracing on slopes. On moderately dry lands farmers should cultivate crops that withstand long spells without rains (millet, sorghum, beans, maize) and allow for regular fallow periods.

Sustainable agriculture can reduce the amount of water usually used in agriculture. Using gravity-flow irrigation systems or trickle-drip irrigation saves water and greatly reduces salinization. Water spreading, control of evaporation through mulching, water harvesting, and no-tillage agriculture are practicable and could be widely adopted.[12]

RESTORATION OF THE ENVIRONMENT

Restoration of eroded land, polluted water, denuded forests, and destroyed coral reefs is an essential part of sustainable development. In the Philippines, for example, on the Island of Mindanao, only 12 percent of the virgin forest remains. A portion of this land is home to the Subanuns, the tribal people who have lived there in a sustainable way for thousands of years (see Chapter 3). Since the 1960s, when logging companies began to cut down the tropical forests, the people have become impoverished, ill, and malnourished. Loss of the tropical forest has caused run-off of the fragile topsoil during heavy rains into mangrove swamps and coral reefs on the coast, as well as siltation of irrigation systems and rice paddies. Today, Columban missionaries working with the Subanuns are helping them to restore the fertility of their soil and plant a variety of trees. The Subanuns' goal is to bring new life to their once lush land.

Projects such as this exist around the world. More and more people are learning about the intricacies of their ecosystems. Some groups have restored degraded wetlands; others have built artificial coral reefs. In some areas rice paddies, which once supported a wide variety of aquatic life but were destroyed by pesticides, have been brought back to their original fertility.

Of course, the greater the complexity of the ecosystem, the greater the difficulty in restoring it. This should make us cautious about degrading nature's processes. Restoration of polluted, running water is perhaps the easiest. Simply discontinuing the flow of pollutants into the waters can allow nature's own system to cleanse itself.

Restoration of soil is possible through traditional methods of soil cultivation. These include simple ways of catching water and holding soil; use of liquid manures, natural fertilizers, and compost; rotation of crops and growing varied crops; and natural pest control.

The restoration of coral reefs and rain forests, however, is possible only over many millennia. Coral reefs take centuries to grow and are very fragile. The coral reef, home to more plant and animal species than any other marine ecosystem, is perhaps the world's oldest ecosystem, surviving intact since the emergence of life on Earth. Reefs generate chemicals useful to humans, including histamines, hormones, and antibiotics. They can teach human beings about symbiotic relationships, helping us to understand connections among plants and animals on land. The destruction of coral reefs through construction, erosion, pollution, sedimentation, tourism, mining, blasting, over-fishing, and nuclear testing is a great tragedy.

The restoration of rain forests, though it takes thousands of years, may depend only on the stopping of human interference and lowering of the density of human population living in them. As we noted earlier, for thousands of years forest dwellers used shifting cultivation methods. Once the poor rain forest soil could no longer support crops the forest dwellers moved on, chopping down trees to create new patches of cleared ground. But they had little impact on the forest; their numbers were few, and the forest surrounding the small cultivated patches remained intact. Therefore, seeds were available for the forest to reestablish itself.

Restoration can be as natural as treating the soil well in gen-erations-old methods. It can also mean a strenuous and, at times, heartbreaking task, that may not, even over many years, succeed. Efforts at restoring natural river courses lie in this category. The outlook is grim for the survival of some ecological systems unless there are many changes in human activity on the Earth. If we accelerate our practice of restoration, we will be well on our way to a sustainable world.

LAND REFORM AND DEVELOPMENT

Few deny that owning one's own land or sharing in the ben-efits of communally owned land, able to pass it on to future generations, is a primary impetus to careful husbandry. Own-ership of land, in addition to literacy, health care, a community's control over common resources, and provision of credit are all basic means of diminishing poverty and environmental destruc-tion.

Governments need to support such efforts, putting the poor first. International efforts are needed to undergird these goals. Aid provided internationally can support land reform and provision of appropriate education and technology for those who work the land.

Compensation paid by more developed countries in return for the protection and sustainable use of natural resources can help developing countries buy up land held in large plantations. These freed land holdings can be returned to individual and family farm holders, who will then be able to grow crops for their own use and local markets. This will protect environmental resources and promote people's self-reliance.

We do not minimize the violence and conflict often attendant upon land redistribution. For this reason, the national government's clear understanding that land reform leads to economic development and environmental protection is mandatory.

ENERGY AND DEVELOPMENT

To develop a sustainable energy system, the world needs to rely on renewable sources of energy, such as wind, hydropower, solar, and so on. In developed countries, renewed efforts at efficiency can curtail energy use by half without diminishing economic stability.[13]

Most of the technology needed for sustainable energy development already exists and will continue to develop during the next decade. Governmental support is indispensable if sustainable energy policies are to be promoted and implemented.

All efforts to develop sustainable energy, however, need to take into account environmental and human factors. Large hydropower projects in Canada, Brazil, and elsewhere have vastly disrupted ecosystems and the lives of indigenous peoples. An ill-conceived government attempt at implementing a series of four hydroelectric dams that would have flooded the ancestral lands and ancient burial grounds of the Kalinga and Bontoc peoples in the Philippines met with open rebellion. To a people whose sacred earth held the bones and memories of their ancestors, the hydro project was no less than an attack upon their spiritual life.

In rural areas people burn fuelwood, dung, brush, rice husks, and millet stalks for energy, particularly to cook food. We have mentioned the depletion of forests through firewood use. A further problem with burning fuel for cooking is smoke, which irritates the eyes and damages the lungs. Many village communities have experimented with improved fuel-efficient cookstoves. These stoves can cook "the same meal with a half or a third of the firewood used by the three-stone stove with a corresponding reduction in smoke."[14] For some poor households, expenditures for fuelwood are higher than those for food; efficient stoves can bring about very significant gains. Fuel-efficient stoves also allow women more time for hoeing or weeding, and potentially for leisure.

There are a variety of other possible sustainable energy technologies for village use. Each has its advantages and drawbacks and needs to be used with a consideration of specific environmental circumstances and village needs. Sustainable technologies already in use for water heating, irrigation, refrigeration, and lighting can be based on solar energy, biogas (methane, produced by heating organic matter), ethanol (ethyl alcohol, made from a wide variety of plants containing sugar or starches), no-dam mini-hydropower, wind power, and others.[15]

The developed world can put itself on a sustainable energy path within the next fifty years if a consistent, enlightened approach is taken. To begin, a carbon tax on all sources of carbon emissions could be levied. Not only would this reflect the true cost of energy sources, but the amounts collected could fund research into sustainable technologies. Conservation can reduce energy use. The California Energy Commission estimates that "cost-effective investments could reduce total U.S. electricity demand by 40-75 percent while improving the quality of life through cleaner air and lower energy costs."[16]

A mixture of technologies, including geothermal, solar, and wind, could then be phased in to put the developed world on a sustainable path. However, in the next few decades, the greatest boost toward clean energy use would be through natural gas. A gas turbine combined cycle plant (in which excess heat fuels the original or a second turbine for enhanced power generation) has a higher conversion efficiency than a coal-fired steam plant. Gas turbine plants emit half the carbon dioxide of coal-fired plants and fewer air-borne pollutants. Natural gas turbine combined cycle systems could be installed at older, inefficient coal and oil gas plants. Natural gas engines could be used in cars once a catalytic converter that removes nitrogen oxide emissions is developed. There is "enough natural gas to double world use of gas during the next 20-30 years and then to sustain that level for at least a couple of decades."[17]

Natural gas, because it is a limited resource and because it produces some global warming gases, would be a stepping stone to the use of hydrogen gas, which would become the main sustainable energy source. Hydrogen can be produced electrolytically, but at a fairly high cost at present. Technological research will lower the costs. In addition, storage technologies and efficiency gains are needed. But hydrogen produced through solar, wind, and natural gas power could meet much of the world's energy needs, creating a clean, sustainable energy system. Furthermore, existing gas pipeline routes, with the pipelines modified, could be used.

Governments should encourage the private sector to work toward a solar hydrogen energy system by setting limits on global warming gases, levying taxes, redirecting military research budgets, and setting policy goals. Thus we provide a climate in which smaller organizations devoted to research and technology development are encouraged to produce designs and marketable products. These organizations, along with electrical utilities, could be competing with each other to produce cost effective, efficient, clean, and sustainable energy technologies needed to carry the world's economies into the twenty-first century and beyond.

CONDITIONS OF PEACE

Sustainable development requires conditions of peace. Relatively small cuts in military spending can free up enormous amounts of money for sustainable development and research toward a healthier environment. Indeed, because environmental damage may well pose the greatest threat to security in the next generation, it is appropriate that military expenditures be redistributed to meet this threat. National armies "should be converted into environmental protection corps, which would monitor and repair damage to natural systems, including clean up of military bases, and be available to assist citizens in times of natural and man-made disasters."[18] Were each country in the western hemisphere to reduce its military expenditures by 20 percent from 1990 levels, $250 billion would be freed for debt reduction and furtherance of environmentally sustainable development programs.

Is renewed hope that human beings can stop waging wars justified? The dire need to work for the communion of human beings living on a finite Earth may help. If we seek peace, based on justice, we then deny many of the falsehoods that lead to war. These include the strong, almost idolatrous support of a nation-state, the clinging to outworn conflicts over political systems (capitalism versus communism, for example), and the belief that trade in arms among countries is a viable economic and political endeavor. We can take hope and example from the people of Japan and Germany who, while not spending exorbitant amounts on arms, have achieved high economic performance. Finally, as we come to understand the whole Earth as a shared resource, a shared gift from God, and as we create just institutions and financial arrangements, some important causes of war will be cut off at their roots.

POPULATION AND DEVELOPMENT

Control of human population is essential to sustainable development. One in three mothers in developing countries wants fewer children but lacks the education, confidence, and contraceptives with which to control her fertility.[19] While many governments around the world support family-planning programs, few are effective. In Africa only two of thirty-two countries surveyed had effective population control programs.[20]

Successful family planning programs build on local traditions. In Kenya, for example, a program relied on the *haram-bee*, or self-help tradition, and traditional family practices such as prolonged breast-feeding. This successful program linked volunteers, nurses, traditional birth attendants, and field educators to impoverished women who desired to limit their families. The direct education of these impoverished mothers was linked to traditional concerns: women's and children's health, and a decrease in infant mortality.

A highly successful program in Zimbabwe has resulted in 38 percent of fertile women using birth control (while in Africa as a whole only 11 percent of all women use any form of birth control). The program had full government support, a strong educational program, and developed 122 clinics staffed by 520 community-based distributors, who reach out to rural areas by bicycle, making contraceptives and advice only thirty-six minutes away from any woman.[21] This form of direct education enables women to make decisions.

We can look at a program instituted by outsiders in the Philippines to see the value of culturally sensitive population control programs. The family-planning program as presented in the Philippines was so culturally offensive to the general populace that it gained little acceptance. It never addressed the Filipino values of giving life or the importance of family. Had the promoters of this program listened to local family-life leaders they could have designed an effective program.

All population policies should include education of men as well as women and should hold them accountable for participation in the progress of family-planning programs. Most people agree that providing opportunities for women and girls that compete with childbearing and childcare slows population growth. The importance of education for women in reducing population is shown in this example from the mountain highlands of Bolivia:

> In the rugged Yungas region north of La Paz, hundreds of impoverished peasants take high school-level courses in market towns when they come to sell their produce. The

curriculum, designed by a dedicated independent group called CETHA to be relevant to local conditions, also offers intensive week-long vocational courses during the agricultural slack season. Most important, the effort has managed to enroll nearly as many women as men. Studies on every continent show that as female literacy rates rise so do income levels, nutrition levels, and child survival rates; at the same time, population growth slows, as women gain the self-confidence to assert control over their bodies.[22]

THE FURTHERING AND ENCOURAGEMENT OF LOCAL DEVELOPMENT INITIATIVE

Paul Harrison tells us in *The Greening of Africa* that no development project will succeed without community involvement and backing and the acceptance of some risk on the part of the people.[23] This makes sense. Projects that develop from local initiative have many advantages over those proposed and managed by outside sources. The primary and most obvious advantage is that projects that come from the local people inspire ownership of and enthusiastic support for the program. The people understand how the project provides attractive alternatives to present ways of doing things and how it will meet their perceived needs.

A second advantage of local initiative is the preservation of local values. As we have seen, for many groups a detailed knowledge of their environment and the ways in which they have learned to live in harmony with their surroundings was interwoven into their cultural and religious world-view. No one can better teach the people of each region about the complex environment in which they live than those who have lived sustainably in that region for many years. Local people also know most about the needs and the abilities of all those in the community. Aware of its knowledge of the environment and its society, a community can then work in partnership with outside planners to design, implement, monitor, and evaluate projects.

Local initiatives in the area of agriculture should rely on appropriate technology that is sustainable in the local conditions and affordable for the local people. Technical support for these initiatives might take the form of assistance in better understanding the scientific rationale behind the local technology, combined with better ways of applying the technology.

Robert Chambers[24] has made a very interesting analysis between "first" (developed) and "last" (undeveloped) values and development projects based on them. "First" development projects as a rule require a large amount of capital and technological expenditures as well as manipulation of social and land patterns. Large dams are an example. They often require the resettlement of indigenous poor people and destroy indigenous ecosystems. They benefit urban or more developed groups that have access to the water through piping or irrigation. Those who benefit financially are often those who hold title to the land (governments and wealthy landowners; almost never the poor or women). The poor stand to lose; in fact, their plight is made even worse in most cases, as they are forced into prefabricated government-owned villages and have to begin again to cultivate the land given to them to work or to find other ways of surviving.

To development professionals used to the "first" approach, sustainable development from the point of view of the "last" approach, from the perspective of the poor, may mean looking at the world from the bottom up. A chart is helpful in showing the differences between the two approaches:

First Values	*Last Values*
Urban	Rural
Industrial	Agricultural
High Cost	Low Cost
Capital-intensive	Labor-intensive
Mechanical	Animal or human
Inorganic	Organic
Large	Small
Modern	Traditional
Exotic	Indigenous

Market	Subsistence
Quantified	Unquantified
Geometrical	Irregular
Visible and seen	Invisible or unseen
Tidy	Untidy
Predictable	Unpredictable
Hard	Soft
Clean	Dirty
Odorless	Smelly

Collaboration between development professionals and local people (between people using "first" and those using "last" values) *can* be helpful if the benefits and limits of each are kept in mind. For example, in Colombia scientists wanted to test the results of the use of phosphate rock and farmers wanted to know the response of various combinations of phosphate rock with chicken manure. The scientists used the statistical ("first") method to test the farmers' ("last") questions.[25]

SELF-RELIANT COMMUNITIES

In order for the human family to live in a sustainable way on the Earth, people seem to need to identify with groups that are smaller than most nation-states. These groups have their own cultural awareness and customs and are capable of developing or nurturing a strong sense of the larger natural ecosystems in which they live.

If we can achieve a sense of place, farm sustainably, and restore ecosystems, we will all stand to gain. Self-reliant groups live in an environmentally sustainable way by meeting their basic needs as much as possible from local resources. They plan for their future, using all their knowledge and love of the environment. They do not concern themselves with competing with other groups for scarce resources or market goods; rather, they have both a healthy respect for their own ways of doing things and an interest in diverse ideals and experiences of other communities.

Self-reliant communities function democratically, with no part of the community left out of decision making. They provide health care and appropriate education to all their members. Local and national governments, as well as nongovernmental organizations (NGOs) and church groups, should support the self-reliance of communities within their territories. Local, national, and regional governments should create infrastructures and services as requested by the communities to enhance their ability to remain self-reliant. Local governments should ensure safe and sufficient water supplies, environmentally sound sewage treatment, and proper waste disposal. The role of governments is to enhance and strengthen the health of the environment and the communities.

As we have noted, governments can ensure that the prices of all products made from natural resources reflect the true value of those resources. With these policies in place, communities can derive benefit from the value of their natural resources and be motivated to preserve them. Governments can help communities to develop long-term economic and social development plans that foster the stability and diversity of the environment. They will support people in living frugally and sustainably and in working in partnership with other communities.

Self-reliant communities continually educate themselves about the environment. Interchange among communities must include exchange of information and technical assistance. A self-reliant community is continually relearning and reassessing its economic and environmental planning in light of its values and goals.

Because the citizens actively participate in creating many aspects of community life, indifference, cynicism, and passivity will be diminished. Environmental destruction caused by unjust economic, social, and political structures and lack of peoples' participation will no longer occur.

The recent growth of peoples' movements and of grassroots NGOs — examples of Chambers's "last" development approach — may be important stages toward more self-reliant communities. In 1976 in Bangladesh Muhammad Yunus distributed small loans to landless villagers to buy basic tools for farming and raw materials. This developed by 1983 into the Grameen (Village) Bank, which now has a million borrowers. One study showed the villagers doubled their income through use of credit from the bank. This program has been highly effective in increasing poor people's access to productive assets.

Grameen's thousands of "bicycle bankers" now wander the alleys and dusty paths of Bangladesh telling the landless about the bank that makes loans to the poor at 16 percent annual interest — a tenth what moneylenders charge. Because the poor lack assets to use as collateral, Grameen has devised an ingenious peer pressure method to ensure repayment. Loan applicants must find four others with whom to apply, and the group is then responsible for ensuring that all members pay. Repayment rates are higher than for any commercial lending program, with only a few percent not meeting their obligations; many actually pay their weekly installments in advance in order to get a second loan sooner. Grameen's clients have augmented their incomes dramatically.[26]

In India, one village wrote its own village land-use program. In a once devastated area in the Aravali hills of the west Indian state of Rajasthan, villagers now live surrounded by lush grass. "Even during the severe drought of 1987, when cattle died by the thousands in neighboring areas, Seed's villagers filled 80 bullock carts with grass."[27]

In Cameroon, supported by the World Wide Fund for Nature, a forest tribal group decided to move to areas called agricultural zones. In these zones roads to markets, schools, and clinics will be built and the native crop production boosted by sustainable agricultural practices. The forest, home to 40 percent of the species on the African continent, will be protected.

On Laguna de Bay in the Philippines (the largest inland lake in Southeast Asia) about seventy thousand people depend upon lake fishing for their existence. In the past twenty years seven hundred factories were built, which pollute the waters, and wealthy entrepreneurs constructed over 100,000 acres of illegal fishing pens. The fishermen complained of decreased fish catches, yet they had little power to change the situation.

Finally, the fishermen organized themselves into fifty-eight associations with the help of the Asian Social Institute Family Center (FCASI). The FCASI helped fishing communities take the initiative in development efforts. Those efforts led to a joint project sponsored and supported by FCASI, CODEL, and other nonprofit groups to train fishermen and their families in ecology, social organization, and leadership. Those trained went out to train others in their communities. The project constructed a fishermen's educational center. The center included a demonstration center for organic farming (including fish ponds), animal raising, agro-forestry, and biogas production from pig manure. A seed bank was developed and a livestock dispersal program launched.

As a result of training, many communities in the area formed ecology committees, which became politically active. The fishermen and their families effectively supported the Fisheries Code (which controls the extent of fishing in coastal waters), sought closure of waters to illegal private and commercial fishing vessels, and protested the dumping in one area of 90 percent of municipal wastes into the lake.

Returning power and land to the people, along with information, credit, and technology with which to create a sustainable life, is the best hope of an environmentally sound future. Replicating this approach many thousands of times around the world, in many different cities and towns, will be necessary. By fostering this development, Christians bring to reality Jesus' teaching that the meek will inherit the Earth.

U.S. farmer and writer Wendell Berry has characterized such communities in this way: "Our present 'leaders'—the people of wealth and power—do not know what it means to take a place seriously: to think it worthy, for its own sake, of life and study and careful work ... The right scale of work gives power to affection ... An adequate local culture, among other things, keeps work within the scope of love."[28]

CONCLUSION

As Christians, it is for us to study and implement ways in which human beings into the far future can live lovingly, joyfully, and peacefully on this Earth. We have listed in this chapter some of the strategies and tactics needed to attain this end. They include new ways of valuing the Earth's resources, land reform, and health and education for all. We emphasized the role of women asserting control over their own lives. International and national policies will foster self-reliance of communities, conditions of peace, and economic policies to enable communities to care for the poor, restore the environment, and diversify economies. We emphasized diversity, with a stress on local initiative and cultural diversity as well as biological diversity. The availability of population control measures is essential. As we shift to sustainable energy paths, we will gain needed knowledge about how the Earth functions. These are concrete activities that flow out of a concern for the Earth and its peoples.

Every human program in some way or another affects the natural environment. Most significant social changes have an impact on the environment. We will be judged by future generations for our care of this planet. Every human effort needs to be critiqued as to whether it ensures the fertility of the soil, the purity of the water sources and watershed areas, the protection of wild lands and plants, and social justice. In a word, every effort needs to be examined as to whether it contributes to environmentally sustainable development.

We challenge Christians to seek out others who are nurturing and healing this fragile planet Earth. Many scientists and others concerned with the environmental crisis and sustainable development recognize the spiritual dimensions of the problem. They call on religious people to provide courageous and joyful leadership. This is our opportunity. Perhaps this is the most effective way to translate into concrete terms the unforgettable vision of Paul, who speaks of a creation which has "been groaning in labor pains until now" (Romans 8:22).

SUGGESTIONS FOR INDIVIDUAL REFLECTION
OR GROUP DISCUSSION

1. Study development policy in your area. Is it environmentally and socially sustainable? Is it just?

2. Evaluate the effects of the military on you, other people, and the environment. What directions would you recommend for the future?

3. List all the aspects that you would include in a measure of a sustainable society (aspects of life you consider important in measuring a country's wealth or well-being). Compare them to the listing given in this chapter. How wealthy would you say your area is?

4. Identify local and global environmental problems that you feel strongly about. Suggest ways to halt destruction of forests, land degradation, water pollution, growth of poverty and powerlessness — whatever you identify as particularly important. Commit yourself to a particular action, after carefully discussing and planning both your goals and steps toward reaching them. Create a litany or prayer service to be used each time you meet to consider further action.

5. Share information about other groups that work for social justice and environmental restoration. Consider ways to be mutually supportive.

APPENDIX 1

Statements from Christian Faith Traditions on Ecology

Although statements have been made by leaders in all major faith traditions about faith and environment, there is not yet anywhere a full integration in practice of faith and ecological stewardship on a large scale. These statements are included to encourage the faithful to move in this direction and to provide resources for reflection and guidelines for action.

(Statements followed by an asterisk can be obtained by writing to CODEL)

ROMAN CATHOLIC

"Companions in Creation"
Catholic Bishops of Florida
January 1991
Florida Catholic Conference
PO Box 1571, Tallahassee, FL 32302 USA

"Renewing the Earth: An Invitation to Reflection and Action on the Environment in Light of Catholic Social Teaching"
United States Bishops
November 1991
Origins, CNS Documentary Service, 12 December 1991, vol. 21, no. 27
3211 4th St., NE, Washington, DC 20017-1100 USA

"Peace with God the Creator, Peace with All of Creation"
Pope John Paul II
January 1990
Walter E. Grazer, U.S. Catholic Conference
3211 4th St., NE, Washington, DC 20017-1194 USA

"Caring for Creation: Our Christian Calling"
Franciscan Communications
1990
1229 S. Santee St., Los Angeles, CA 90015 USA

"The Ecological Crisis"
Federation of Asian Bishops' Conferences
July 1989
Office for Human Development
Dona Matilde Building, R-301 876 G Apacible
Ermita Manila, PO Box 1446, Manila, Philippines

"Ecology: The Bishops of Lombardy Address the Community"
The Catholic Bishops of Northern Italy
November 1989
North American Conference on Christianity and Ecology
PO Box 14305, San Francisco, CA 94114 USA

"Solidarity with the Poor in Ecological Perspective"
Columban Fathers General Assembly
1989
PO Box 10, St. Columbans, Nebraska 68056 USA

"Crying Out for the Land: Collective Pastoral Letter of the Bishops
Conference of Guatemala"*
February, 1988

"What Is Happening to Our Beautiful Land?"
Catholic Bishops Conference of the Philippines
July 1988
Lingkod Tao Kalikasan
c/o Sister Ma. Aida Velasquez OSB
PO Box 2734, Manila, 1089 Philippines

"An Appeal to Governments in the Pacific"
Catholic Bishops Conference of the Pacific

July 1988
Federation of Asian Bishops' Conferences
Office of Human Development
Dona Matilde Building, R-301 876 G Apacible
Ermita Manila, PO Box 1446, Manila, Philippines

"La Relacion del Hombre con la Naturaleza"
Carta Pastoral/Conferencia del Episcopado Dominicano
January 1987
Progressio, Fundacion para el Mejoramiento Humano
Edif. de la Asociacion Popular de Ahorros y Prestamos
Av. Maximo Gomez esq. Av. 27 de Febrero, piso 3
Santo Domingo, Republica Dominicana

"Report on Food and Agriculture"
United States Bishops
November 1986
Origins, CNS Documentary Service, 1 December 1988, vol. 18, no. 25
3211 4th St., NE, Washington, DC 20017-1100 USA

PROTESTANT AND ECUMENICAL

"The YWCA Energy and Environment Newsletter"
World YWCA (Young Women's Christian Organization)
37 Quai Wilson, 1201 Geneva, Switzerland

"Towards an Ecological Worldview for the Mission of the Church"
The National Council of Churches in India
1990
Christian Council Lodge
Nagpur 440 001
Maharashtra 531312 India

"101 Ways to Help Save the Earth"
Eco-Justice Working Group
The National Council of Churches of Christ
1990
475 Riverside Drive, Room 572, New York, NY 10115 USA

"Alverna Covenant," "Caretakers Packet" (updated annually)
Christian Church (Disciples of Christ)
Robert F. Glover, Task Force on Christian Life Style and Ecology
PO Box 1986, Indianapolis, IN 46206 USA

"To Encourage Environmental Stewardship"
The Lutheran Church, Missouri Synod
July 1992
David Mahsman
1333 S. Kirkwood Rd., St. Louis, MO 63122-7295 USA

"Environmental Stewardship," "Toxic Waste and Race," "The Law of
the Sea," "Energy" (1988)
"Environmental Justice for a Sustainable Future," "Environmental
Racism" (1992)
United Methodist Church, U.S.A.
Maria Paz Artaza or Jaydee Hanson
General Board of Church and Society
100 Maryland Avenue, NE, Washington DC 20003 USA

"Caring for Creation: Vision, Hope, and Justice"
Evangelical Lutheran Church of America
1992 (draft, final document expected September, 1993)
Job S. Ebeneezer
Office for Studies, Division for Church in Society
8765 W. Higgins Road, Chicago, IL 60631 USA

"Creation: Called To Care"
Church of the Brethren
July 1991
1451 Dundee Avenue, Elgin IL 60120 USA

"1991 General Convention Environmental Resolutions"
Episcopal Church
Ethan Flad, Environment and Special Projects
The Episcopal Church Center, 815 Second Ave.
New York, NY 10017

"Advocating for Ecological Wholeness and Racial Justice"
"Resolution on Individual Lifestyle for Ecological Responsibility"
"American Baptist Policy Statement on Ecology"
"Our Only Home, Planet Earth" (prayer and Bible study guide based
on policy statement - $3 [U.S.]/copy)
American Baptist Churches, USA
1990
Owen Owens, PO Box 851, Valley Forge, PA 19482-0851 USA

"Restoring Creation for Ecology and Justice: A Report of the 202nd General Assembly of the Presbyterian Church (U.S.A.)"
June 1990
Office of Environmental Justice
The Rev. Bill Somplatsky-Marman
100 Witherspoon Street, Louisville, KY 40202-1396 USA

"Integrity of Creation, Justice and Peace Packet," which includes "Redeeming Creation: Relating Redemption Theology and Creation Theology as a Basis for Relating Justice and Peace Advocacy to Environment Advocacy," "Wellspring Covenant"
United Church of Christ
1990
Pat Conover, Office of Church in Society
110 Merlin Avenue, NE, Washington DC 20002 USA

"Toxic Waste and Race in the United States"
United Church of Christ Commission on Racial Justice
475 Riverside Drive, Room 1950, New York, NY USA

"Justice, Peace, and the Integrity of Creation: An Open Letter to the Children and Young People of the Planet"
World Alliance of Reformed Churches General Assembly Korea
August 1989
150 Route de Ferney, 1211 Geneva 2, Switzerland

"Stewardship of the Earth: Resolution on Environment and Faith Issues"
Mennonite Church
August 1989
MBCM, Box 1245, Elkhart, Indiana 46515 USA

"Resolution on the World Food Crisis"
Mennonite Central Committee, U.S.A. and Canada
Adopted, 1974, and Reaffirmed, 1984
21 South 12th Street, Box M, Akron, PA 17501 USA

"A Reformed Theology of Nature in a Crowded World" (1970)
"Care for the Earth: Theology and Practice" (1982)
Reformed Church in America
John Paarlberg, 475 Riverside Drive, 18th floor
New York, NY 10115 USA

"Public Policy Statement on the Environment"
Unitarian Universalist Association (1971)
Unitarian Universalist Service Committee (1975)
Mary Lania, International Programs
130 Prospect Street, Cambridge, MA 02139-1845

ORTHODOX

"Orthodoxy and the Ecological Crisis" (includes the pastoral message
of the Patriarch on this topic)
September 1990
Greek Orthodox Archdiocese of North and South America
Rev. Dr. Milton Efthymiou
8-10 E. 79th Street, New York, NY 10021 USA

WORLD COUNCIL OF CHURCHES

"Searching for the New Heavens and the New Earth: An Ecumenical
Response to UNCED"
1992

"Come Holy Spirit, Renew the Face of the Earth"
January 1991

"Justice, Peace and the Integrity of Creation"
March 1990

"Caring for Creation: Call to the Latin American Churches"
World Council of Churches and Universidad Estatal a Distancia
Costa Rica
July 1988

"Reintegrating God's Creation"
September 1987
The World Council of Churches
150 Route de Ferney, PO Box 66 or Box 2100,
1211 Geneva 20, Switzerland

INTERFAITH

"Preserving and Cherishing the Earth: An Appeal for Joint Commitment in Science and Religion"*

Global Forum of Spiritual and Parliamentary Leaders
Moscow
(signed by 32 scientists and 270 spiritual leaders)
January 1990

"The Assisi Declarations: A Call"
Buddhist, Christian, Hindu, Jewish, and Moslem Statements on Nature
World Wide Fund for Nature (WWF), Assisi
September 1986
1196, Gland, Switzerland

APPENDIX 2

Statements on Ecology from Four World Religions

Given at the World Wildlife Federation's Twenty-fifth Anniversary Celebration, Assisi, Italy

EXCERPTS FROM THE ASSISI BUDDHIST DECLARATION

Buddhism is a religion of love, understanding and compassion and is committed towards the ideal of non-violence. As such it also attaches great importance towards wildlife and the protection of the environment on which every being in this world depends for survival.

The underlying reason why beings other than humans need to be taken into account is that, like human beings, they too are sensitive to happiness and suffering. We should therefore be wary of justifying the right of any species to survive solely on the basis of its usefulness to human beings.

We regard our survival as an undeniable right; as coinhabitants of this planet, other species too have this right for survival. And since human beings as well as other non-human sentient beings depend upon the environment as the ultimate source of life and well-being, let us share the conviction that the conservation of the environment, the restoration of the imbalance caused by our negligence in the past, be implemented with courage and determination.

—The Venerable Lungrig Nomgayal

EXCERPTS FROM THE ASSISI HINDU DECLARATION

Not only in the Vedas, but in the later scriptures such as the Upanishads, the Puranas and subsequent texts, the Hindu viewpoint on nature has been clearly enunciated. It is permeated by a reverence for life, and an awareness that the great forces of nature — the earth, the sky, the air, the water and fire — as well as various orders of life including plants and trees, forests and animals are all bound to each other within the great rhythms of nature. The divine is not exterior to creation, but expresses itself through natural phenomena.

In addition, according to the Vaishnava tradition, the evolution of life on this planet is symbolized by a series of divine incarnations beginning with fish, moving through amphibious forms and mammals, and then on into human incarnations. This view clearly holds that man did not spring fully formed to dominate lesser life forms, but rather evolved out of these forms, and is therefore integrally linked to the whole of creation. This leads necessarily to a reverence for animal life.

From the Jains, Ahimsa, or non-violence, is the greatest good, and on no account should life be taken. This philosophy was emphasized more recently by Mahatma Gandhi who always spoke of the importance of Ahimsa and looked upon the cow as a symbol of the benign element of animal life. All this strengthens the attitude of reverence for all life including animals and insects.

The Hindu tradition of reverence for nature and all forms of life, vegetable or animal, represents a powerful tradition which needs to be re-nurtured and re-applied in our contemporary context. Let us recall the ancient Hindu dictum — "The earth is our mother, and we are all her children."

— Doctor Karan Singh

EXCERPTS FROM THE ASSISI MOSLEM DECLARATION

Unity, trusteeship and accountability, that is, *tawheed*, *khalifa*, and *akbrah*, the three central concepts of Islam, are also the pillars of the environmental ethics of Islam. They constitute the basic values taught by the Qur'an. It is these values which led Muhammad, the Prophet of Islam, to say: "Whoever plants a tree and diligently looks after it until it matures and bears fruit is rewarded," and "If a Moslem plants a tree or sows a field and men and beasts and birds eat from it, all of it is charity on his part," and again, "The world is green and beautiful and God has appointed you his stewards over it." Environmental consciousness is born when such values are adopted and become an intrinsic part of our mental and physical makeup.

Moslems need to return to this nexus of values, this way of understanding themselves and their environment. The notions of unity, trusteeship and accountability should not be reduced to matters of personal piety; they must guide all aspects of life and work. If we use these same values, the same understanding in our work as a scientist and technologist, economist or politician as we do to know ourselves as Moslems ... we will create a true Islamic alternative ... to the environmentally destructive thought and action which dominate the world today.

—Doctor Abdullah Omar Nassef

EXCERPTS FROM THE ASSISI JEWISH DECLARATION

The encounter of God and man in nature is conceived in Judaism as a seamless web with man as the leader, and custodian, of the natural world. Even in the many centuries when Jews were most involved in their own immediate dangers and destiny, this universalist concern has never withered ... Now, when the whole world is in peril, when the environment is in danger of being poisoned, and various species, both plant and animal, are becoming extinct, it is our Jewish responsibility to put the defense of the whole of nature at the very center of our concern ... Man was given dominion over nature, but he was commanded to behave towards the rest of creation with justice and compassion. Man lives, always, in tension between his power and the limits set by conscience.

—Rabbi Arthur Hertzberg

APPENDIX 3

A New Decalogue

I the Lord am the God that made you; and as I made you, so have I made all living things, and a fit place for each living thing, and a world for all living things to share in interdependence.

And my reason for making all these are one with my reasons for making you; that each living thing may rejoice in its own being, and in the company of all beings, and in me the sum and essence and fulfillment of being, whose name is I AM THAT I AM: and that I may rejoice in each living thing, and in the company of all living things, which I have blest and hallowed with my love and to which I have lent a measure of that light by which you know that I am near.

All living things I have included in that covenant I made with your ancestors long ago; and by that covenant I gave them rights and a place, which you must not deny them, lest you displease your God.

And so that my creation may be cherished, and my covenant honoured, and my love made manifest, and you regain sight of who you truly are thus I command:

You shall not act in ignorance of the ecological consequence of your acts.

You shall not seek such ignorance, nor hide in such ignorance, hoping to say afterwards, "Forgive me, for I knew not what I did" ...

You shall not keep others in ignorance of the ecological consequences of their acts; for their ecological wrongdoing will be reckoned against you as if it were your own.

> You shall not act in any way which makes the world less
>   able to sustain life:
> not by destroying the soil,
> not by destroying the living seas,
> not by laying waste the wild places,
> not by releasing poisons,
> nor by causing great changes in the climate.

You shall not act in any way that injures the buffers I have set about this world to protect its life;

> the ozone layer of the atmosphere,
> the carbon dioxide sink of the sea,
> the chemical balance of the waters,
> the interface between water and sky,
> the vegetative cover of hillside and plain,
> the multitude of species in a region,
> the balance of species, each with each,
> the adaptability of species, as contained in their genes.

You shall not encroach on a species' niche, or destroy its natural defenses, or reduce its numbers to the point where its survival is endangered.

And as I forbid these acts to you, so I forbid you to place others in a position where they must commit such acts; for their ecological wrongdoing will be reckoned against you as if it were your own.

I am the creator of the world; treasure it as your Father's treasure.

> Honour the life of all living beings,
> and the order of nature, and the wildness of the wilderness,
> and the richness of the created world,
> and the beauty of lands undefiled by your works;
> and seek the holiness I have placed in these things,
> and measure of light I have lent them;
> and preserve these things well;

for these are my gifts to you from the dawn of time,
and their life will not be offered to you again.

And in the fulfillment of these commandments, be not half-hearted,
and do not err on the side of your greed and your convenience: but act
with all your ability to love,

and all your ability to discern;
and all your ability to understand,
and all your ability to foresee;

for I know your capacities, and I will know how well you use them.

And if you will listen carefully to my voice, and accept my guidance in
these matters, and obey and honour and fulfil these commandments,
not in the letter only but in the fullness of truth,

then I will bless your life,
and the lives of all about you,
and all that you hold dear.

I will bless you in your rising and your mid-day and your evening, and
bless your sleep and sweeten all your dreaming;

I will bless your settlements and your cultivations and the wild places
you will never see;

I will add to your riches and multiply your happiness;

From generation to generation you will witness the unfolding of the
future I myself have planned for the world from the beginning of time,
and your hearts will overflow with the joy of it.

But if you will not attend to me, and instead live contrary to my way,
your own acts and choices will become the means of your undoing.

Then it will seem to you that all the world has hardened and turned
against you, though it is only that you have cast yourself out of the
covenant of the world;

Famine and thirst, drought and flood and storm, blight and plague,
division and strife, and slow painful death will walk among you;

Your house will be cast down, your fields laid waste, and all memory of your existence blotted out.

And on the day these punishments arrive, do not think to bargain with the Lord for mercy; for these punishments will come out of the laws I established at the dawn of time, the very laws through which I made you a place in my creation: and these laws are part of the covenant, which I have pledged never to set aside.

Therefore be holy, as I who love you and dwell within you am holy, I am the Lord.

> Marshall Massey, "Uniting Friends with Nature" (talk given at Mount View Meeting, Denver, CO), *Friends Bulletin* (1985), as found in Sean McDonagh, *The Greening of the Church* (Maryknoll, NY: Orbis Books, 1992). Reprinted by permission.

APPENDIX 4

Earth Covenant

A Citizen's Treaty for Common Ecological Security

PREAMBLE

We, the peoples of the Earth, rejoice in the beauty and wonder of the lands, skies, waters, and life in all its diversity. Earth is our home. We share it with all other living beings.

Yet we are rendering the Earth uninhabitable for the human community and for many species of life. Lands are becoming barren, skies fouled, waters poisoned. The cry of people whose land, livelihood, and health are being destroyed is heard around the world. The Earth itself is calling us to awaken.

We and all living beings depend upon the Earth and upon one another for our common existence, well-being, and development. Our common future depends upon a reexamination of our most basic assumptions about humankind's relationship to the Earth. We must develop common principles and systems to shape this future in harmony with the Earth.

Governments alone cannot secure the environment. As citizens of the world, we accept responsibility in our personal, occupational, and community lives to protect the integrity of the Earth.

PRINCIPLES AND COMMITMENTS

In covenant with each other and on behalf of the whole Earth community, we commit ourselves to the following principles and actions:

* *Relationship with the Earth*: All Life forms are sacred. Each human being is a unique and integral part of the Earth's community of life and has a special responsibility to care for life in all its diverse forms.

Therefore, we will act and live in a way that preserves the natural life processes of the Earth and respects all species and their habitats. We will work to prevent ecological degradation.

* *Relationship with Each Other*: Each human being has the right to a healthful environment and to access to the fruits of the Earth. Each also has a continual duty to work for the realization of these rights for present and future generations.

Therefore—concerned that every person have food, shelter, pure air, potable water, education, employment, and all that is necessary to enjoy the full measure of human rights—we will work for more equitable access to the Earth's resources.

* *Relationship between Economic and Ecological Security*: Since human life is rooted in the natural processes of the Earth, economic development, to be sustainable, must preserve the life-support systems of the Earth.

Therefore, we will use environmentally protective technologies and promote their availability to people in all parts of the Earth. When doubtful about the consequences of economic goals and technologies on the environment, we will allow an extra margin of protection for nature.

* *Governance and Ecological Security*: The protection and enhancement of life on Earth demand adequate legislative, administrative, and judicial systems at appropriate local, national, regional, and international levels. In order to be effective, these systems must be empowering, participatory, and based on openness of information.

Therefore, we will work for the enactment of laws that protect the environment and promote their observance through educational, political, and legal action. We shall advance policies of prevention rather than only reacting to ecological harm.

Declaring our partnership with one another and with our Earth, we give our word of honor to be faithful to the above commitments.

———————————————————

(Signature)

- - - - - -

I have signed the Earth Covenant, committing myself with others around the Earth to live an ecologically responsible life. Please enter my signature and address (below) in the Register of Signatories to the Earth Covenant.

_____   _____
(Signature)   (Print Full Name)

_____
(Street Address)

_____   _____
(City)   (State)   (Zip)   (Country)

PLEASE DETACH THIS FORM ON DOTTED LINE AND RETURN TO:

Earth Covenant — c/o Global Education Associates
475 Riverside Drive
Suite 1848
New York, NY 10115, USA

(212)870-3290

APPENDIX 5

For Further Reading on Faith, Ecology, and Development

SUSTAINABLE DEVELOPMENT

Asian NGO Coalition for Agrarian Reform and Rural Development. *People's Participation and Environmentally Sustainable Development.* ANGOC Secretariat, 47 Matrinco Building, 2178 Pasong Tamo, Makati, Metro Manila, Philippines.

Clark, Mary E. *Ariadne's Thread.* St. Martin's Press, 1989. 175 Fifth Ave., New York, NY 10010.

Freudenberger, C. Dean. *Food for Tomorrow?* Minneapolis: Augsburg Publishing House, 1984. 426 S. Fifth Street, Box 1209, Minneapolis, MN 55440.

Global Tomorrow Coalition. *Sustainable Development and How to Achieve It.* 1986. 1325 G St. N.W., Washington, DC 20003.

International Institute of Rural Reconstruction (IIRR) *Agroforestry Technology Information Kit, Regenerative Agriculture Technologies, Resource Book on Sustainable Agriculture for the Uplands, Bio-Intensive Gardening, Aquaculture Training Kit.*
　　Order from: IIRR, 475 Riverside Drive, Room 1270, New York, NY 10115, U.S.A.
　　or: IIRR, Silang, Cavite, Philippines 4118.

Maathai, Wangari. *The Greenbelt Movement: Sharing the Approach and the Experience.* Environment Liaison Centre International, 1988. PO Box 72461, Nairobi, Kenya.

World Commission on Environment and Development. *Our Common*

Future. Oxford University Press, 1987. 200 Madison Ave., New York, NY 10016.

World Resources Institute. *Participatory Rural Appraisal Handbook.* Center for International Development and Environment, 1990. 1709 New York Avenue, NW, Washington DC 20006, U.S.A.

ENVIRONMENT — GENERAL

Brown, Lester R. et al. *State of the World.* New York: W.W. Norton, 1991. 500 Fifth Avenue, New York, NY 10110 (published yearly since 1984).

Durning, Alan. *Poverty and the Environment.* Worldwatch Paper 92. Worldwatch Institute, 1989. 1776 Mass. Ave, N.W., Washington, DC 20036.

Myers, Norman, ed. *GAIA: An Atlas of Planet Management.* Doubleday, 1987. Bantam Doubleday Dell, Fulfillment Dept., 2451 S. Wolf Rd., Des Plaines, IL 60018.

Nash, Roderick. *The Rights of Nature.* University of Wisconsin Press, 1989. 114 N. Murray St., Madison, WI 53715.

ENVIRONMENTAL DESTRUCTION

Brown, Lester and Jodi L. Jacobson. *Our Demographically Divided World.* Worldwatch Paper 74. Worldwatch Institute, 1986. 1776 Mass. Ave., NW, Washington, DC 20036.

Luoma, Jon R. "Forests Are Dying But Is Acid Rain Really to Blame?" *Audubon Magazine,* March 1987. The National Audubon Society, 700 Broadway, New York, NY 10003.

Managing Pests and Pesticides in Small-Scale Agriculture. TOOL, 1989. Sarphatistraat 650, 1018 AV Amsterdam, The Netherlands.

Maslow, Jonathan Evan. *Bird of Life, Bird of Death: A Naturalist's Journey Through a Land of Political Turmoil.* Simon & Schuster, 1986. 1230 Ave. of the Americas, New York, NY 10020.

The Pesticide Handbook: Profiles for Action. International Organization of Consumers Union, 1991. PO Box 1045, 10830 Penan, Malaysia.

ENVIRONMENT AND SPIRITUALITY

Austin, Richard Cartwright. *Environmental Theology.* 4 vols. Creekside Press. PO Box 331, Abingdon, VA 24210.

Berry, Thomas. *The Dream of the Earth.* Sierra Club, 1988. 730 Polk St., San Francisco, CA 94109.

Busch, Vincent. *Hope for the Seeds*. Claretian Publications, 1989. U.P.P.O. Box 4, Diliman, Quezon City, 3004, Philippines.

Fox, Matthew. *Original Blessing: A Primer in Creation Spirituality*. Bear & Company, 1983. PO Drawer 2860, Santa Fe, NM 87504-2860.

Gore, Al. *Earth in the Balance: Ecology and the Human Spirit*. Houghton Mifflin, 1992. 1 Beacon St., Boston, MA 02108.

Granberg-Michaelson, Wesley. *A Worldly Spirituality*. HarperCollins, 1984. 1160 Battery St., San Francisco, CA 94111. (out of print)

Hall, Douglas John. *Imaging God: Dominion as Stewardship*. Eerdmans & Friendship Press, 1986. 255 Jefferson Ave., S.E. Grand Rapids, MI 49503.

Hart, John. *The Spirit of the Earth: A Theology of the Land*. Paulist Press, 1984. 997 Macarthur Blvd., Mahwah, NJ 07430.

Hessel, Dieter T., ed. *After Nature's Revolt: Eco-Justice and Theology*. Augsburg-Fortress, 1992. 4700 Wissahickon Ave., Philadelphia, PA 19144.

Joronson, Philip N., and Ken Butigan. *Cry of the Environment: Rebuilding the Christian Creation Tradition*. Bear & Co., 1984. PO Drawer 2860, Santa Fe, NM 87504-2860.

Lutheran World Federation. *I Have Heard the Cry of My People* (Study Book for the Eighth Assembly). 150 Route de Ferney, PO Box 2100, 1211 Geneva 2, Switzerland.

McDaniel, Jay B. *Of God and Pelicans: A Theology of Reverence for Life*. Westminster/John Knox, 1989. 100 Witherspoon St., Louisville, KY 40202-1396.

McDonagh, Sean, and Vincent Busch. *Our Future Mirage: Theological Reflection on Philippine Ecology*. Claretian Publications, 1986. U.P.P.O. Box 4, Quezon City, Philippines.

McDonagh, Sean. *To Care for the Earth: A Call to a New Theology*. Santa Fe: Bear & Co., 1986. PO Drawer 2860, Santa Fe, NM 87504-2860.

McFague, Sallie. *Models of God: Theology for an Ecological, Nuclear Age*. Fortress, 1987. 4700 Wissahickon Avenue, Philadelphia, PA 19144.

Swimme, Brian and Thomas Berry. *The Universe Story*. HarperCollins, 1992. 10 E. 53rd St., New York, NY 10022

TECHNOLOGY

Gamser, Matthew S., Helen Appleton, and Nicola Carter (eds.). *Tinker, Tiller, Technical Change*. London: Intermediate Technology Publications, 1990. The Bootstrap Press, 777 United Nations Plaza, New York, NY 10017.

Technology As If Tomorrow Mattered. Approtech Asia/CODEL, 1993. CODEL, 475 Riverside Dr., Rm. 1842, New York, NY 10115.

ECONOMICS

Daly, Herman E., and John B. Cobb. *For the Common Good.* Beacon Press, 1989. 25 Beacon Street, Boston, MA 02108-2800.
The Other Economic Summit. *The Living Economy: A New Economics in the Making.* Routledge, Chapman & Hall, Inc., 1986. 29 W. 35th St., New York, NY 10007.

WOMEN

Asian Pacific Development Centre. *Women's Resource and Action Series.* 2 vols. *Health,* 1989; *Environment,* 1992. Presiaran Duta, PO Box 12224, 50770 Kuala Lampur, Malaysia.
Dankelman, Irene, and Joan Davidson. *Women and Environment in the Third World: Alliance for the Future.* Earthscan Publications LTD., 1988. 3 Endsleigh Street, London WCIH OCCC, United Kingdom.
Merchant, Carolyn. *The Death of Nature: Women, Ecology, and the Scientific Revolution.* HarperCollins, 1983. 10 E. 53rd St., New York, NY 10022.
Shiva, Vandana. *Staying Alive: Women, Ecology, and Development.* Zed Books LTD., 1989. 57 Caledonian Road, London NI 9BU, England.
————. *Biodiversity: Social and Ecological Consequences.* Zed Books LTD., 1991. 57 Caledonian Road, London NI 9BU, England.

IMPORTANT DOCUMENTS

Population Reference Bureau, *World Population Data Sheet* (Washington DC, 1986). Published annually.
World Charter for Nature. 1972. Obtain from United Nations Environment Program, Room DC2-0803, New York, NY 10017.

List of CODEL Books and Workshop Reports.

CODEL-VITA Guidelines for Planning Series:
    Environmentally Sound Small-Scale Projects —
    Agriculture (English, Spanish) (1st edition available in French)
    Energy (English)
    Forestry (English, French, Spanish)

Livestock (English, French, Spanish)
Water (English, Spanish)

Unpublished Papers and Reports by CODEL (Selected)

Agroforestry Systems in Zimbabwe: Promoting Trees in Agriculture, A Report on the National NGO Workshop on Agroforestry, Nyanga, Zimbabwe, June 1987.

Environment and Development: A Conference Report, Puncak Pass, West Java, Indonesia, March 1989.

Environment and Development in Central America, Promoting Natural Resource Management in Community-Based Development, A Retrospective of CODEL Strategy, Honduras 1981-1983 (English, Spanish).

Environment and Development in South and Southeast Asia. Report on CODEL Consultation with Nongovernmental Organizations, Bangkok, Thailand, May 1988.

Integration of Programs for Managing Renewable Natural Resources for Human Development, CODEL Workshop, San Jose de Ocoa, Dominican Republic, January 1984 (English, Spanish).

Organic Farming in Kenya. A Report on a National Workshop for Kenya Nongovernmental Organizations, Limuru, Kenya, 1990.

People for Forests. A Report on the Tropical Forestry Workshop, Puncak Pass, West Java, Indonesia, March 1989.

Peoples Participation in Development and the Management of Natural Resources, CODEL Workshop, Vieux Fort, St. Lucia, April 1985.

Select Resources for Relating Environment and Development (Bibliography and Institutional Listing).

CODEL, INC.
Environment and Development Program
475 Riverside Drive, Room 1842
New York, NY 10115

INTERNATIONAL RESOURCE AGENCIES

Cultural Survival, 11 Divinity Avenue, Cambridge, MA 02138.

Environment and Development in the Third World (EDNA), B.P. 3370, Dakar, Senegal.

Environment Liaison Centre International, PO Box 72461, Nairobi, Kenya (a global coalition for environment and development).

The Intermediate Technology Development Group (ITDG), Myson House, Railway Power, Cheltenham, Glos. GL54 5TZ, United Kingdom.

International Centre for Conservation Education, Greenfield House, Guiting Power, Cheltenham, Glos. GL54 5TZ, United Kingdom.

International Council for Research in Agroforestry (ICRAF), PO Box 30677, Nairobi, Kenya.

International Institute for Environment and Development. IIED/ EARTHSCAN is an international organization established to focus attention on sustainable development, or the connections that exist between economic development, the environment, and human needs, particularly in the Third World. It has offices in:

Europe
3 Endsleigh Street
London WCIH ODD
England
Tel. 01-388-2117

North America
1717 Massachusetts Avenue, NW
Washington, DC 20036
USA
Tel. 202-638-6300

Latin America
Corrientes 2835, 7 piso
1193 Buenos Aires
Argentina
Tel. 541-87-2355

International Institute of Rural Reconstruction (IIRR), Silang, Cavite, Philippines.

International Organization of Consumers Unions, PO Box 1045, 10830 Penang, Malaysia.

International Union for the Conservation of Nature and Natural Resources, 1196 Gland, Switzerland.

International Women's Tribune Centre, 777 United Nations Plaza, New York, NY 10017.

United Nations Development Programme (UNDP), DC 1, United Nations, New York, NY 10017.

United Nations Environment Programme (UNEP), DC 2, United Nations, New York, N.Y. 10117. (Supports an inter-faith Environmental Sabbath, celebrated each year on World Environment Day, with supporting free materials.)

The World Conservation Union, Avenue du Mont-Blanc, CH-1196 Gland, Switzerland.

World Council of Churches, Justice, Peace, and the Integrity of Creation Programme, 150 Route de Ferney, Geneva, Switzerland.

World Resources Institute, 1735 New York Avenue, NW, Washington, DC 20006.

World Wildlife Fund, 1250 Twenty-fourth Street, NW, Washington, DC 20037.

World Wide Fund for Nature, International CH-1196 Gland, Switzerland (includes a strong interfaith ecology and spirituality program).

NOTES

CHAPTER 1: HEARING THE CRY OF THE POOR

1. Alan B. Durning, *Worldwatch Paper 92: Poverty and the Environment, Reversing the Downward Spiral* (Washington, DC: Worldwatch Institute, 1989), p. 27.
2. Ibid. pp. 41-42.
3. Ibid. p. 62.
4. Erik P. Eckholm, *Down To Earth* (New York: W. W. Norton & Company, 1982), p. 37.
5. Paul Harrison, *The Greening of Africa* (London: Paladin Grafton Books, 1987), p. 244.
6. *Understanding the Presbyterian Hunger Program*, 100 Witherspoon Street, Louisville, KY 40202.
7. *Hunger: Myths and Realities*, Office of Global Education, Church World Service, 2115 N. Charles Street, Baltimore, MD 21218-5755. This FACT sheet is one in a series, each covering a facet of global education.
8. Durning, *Poverty and the Environment*, p. 30.
9. Sean McDonagh, *The Greening of the Church* (Maryknoll, NY: Orbis Books, 1990), p. 43.
10. Irene Dankelman and Joan Davidson, *Women and Environment in the Third World* (London: Earthscan Publications Ltd., 1988), p. 68.
11. Ibid., p. 69.
12. Durning, *Poverty and the Environment*, p. 22.
13. Norman Myers, *GAIA: An Atlas of Planet Management* (Garden City, NY: Anchor Books, 1984), p. 120.
14. Durning, *Poverty and the Environment*, p. 22.
15. Ibid. p. 16.
16. Ibid. pp. 9-11.
17. Robert McNamara, a former president of the World Bank, quoted in Myers, *GAIA*, p. 220.
18. James Gustave Speth, "A Post-Rio Compact," *Foreign Policy* 88 (Fall 1992): 149.

19. Environmental Liaison Centre International, *International Environment and Development File*, June/Sept. 1991, p. 14.

20. Durning, *Poverty and the Environment*, p. 35.

CHAPTER 2: THE ENVIRONMENTAL CRISIS

1. Norman Myers, *GAIA: An Atlas of Planet Management* (Garden City, NY: Anchor Books, 1984), p. 48.

2. Lester Brown, *State of the World 1990* (Washington DC: Worldwatch Institute, 1990), p. 64.

3. Myers, *GAIA*, p. 41.

4. Ibid., p. 156.

5. Ibid. p. 42.

6. Thomas Berry, *The Dream of the Earth* (San Francisco: Sierra Club, 1988), p. 9.

7. UNEP Media Release, 5 May 1992.

8. For further information on rain forests, see Catherine Caufield, *In The Rain Forest* (New York: Alfred A. Knopf, 1985); Jonathan Evan Maslow, *Bird of Life, Bird of Death: A Naturalist's Journey Through a Land of Political Turmoil* (New York: Simon & Schuster, 1986).

9. UNEP Media Release, 5 May 1992.

10. Lester Brown, *State of the World 1992* (Washington: Worldwatch Institute, 1992), pp. 32-33.

11. Lester Brown, *State of the World 1991* (Washington: Worldwatch Institute, 1991), pp. 21, 23.

12. Ibid. pp. 21-22.

13. Ibid. p. 24.

14. Irene Dankelman and Joan Davidson, *Women and Environment in the Third World* (London: Earthscan Publications Ltd., 1988), p. 69.

15. Alan B. Durning, *Worldwatch Paper 92: Poverty and the Environment, Reversing the Downward Spiral* (Washington, DC: Worldwatch Institute, 1989), p. 67.

16. See Sandra Postel, *Worldwatch Paper 71: Altering the Earth's Chemistry: Assessing the Risks* (Washington, DC: Worldwatch Institute, July 1986).

17. UNEP Media Release, 5 May 1991.

18. See Paul Brodeur, "Annals of Chemistry (The Ozone Layer)," *The New Yorker*, 9 June 1986, pp. 70-87.

19. Myers, *GAIA*, p. 244.

20. Ibid. p. 246.

21. Gerard Manley Hopkins, *Selected Poems and Prose*, ed. W. H. Gardner (New York: Penguin, 1963), pp. 39-40.

CHAPTER 3: INDIGENOUS PEOPLE AND THE EARTH

1. The authors are indebted to Dr. John Grim for helping them understand the world-views of indigenous people. Grim authored *The Shaman* (Norman: University of Oklahoma Press, 1983). For further reading on indigenous peoples' cosmological world-view and the diversity of indigenous cultures, see, on Africa, Marc R. Schloss, *The Hatchet's Blood: Separation, Power, and Gender in Ehing Social Life* (Tucson: University of Arizona Press, 1988); on Australian aboriginal peoples, Diane Bell, *Daughters of the Dreaming* (Winchester, MA: Unwin Hyman, Inc., 1984); on New Guinea, Roy Rappaport, *Pigs for the Ancestors: Ritual in the Ecology of a New Guinea People* (New Haven: Yale University Press, 1984); and on the North American Indians, Richard Nelson, *Make Prayers to the Raven* (Chicago: University of Chicago Press, 1983).

2. Nelson, *Make Prayers to the Raven*, p. 245.

3. "Dawn Boy's Song on Entering White House," in Philip Hyde and Stephen C. Jett, *Navajo Wildlands* (New York: Sierra Club and Ballantine Books, 1969), p. 98.

4. From a paper by Hans van den Berg, O.S.A., *"Conviven con la Tierra,"* *Cuarto Intermedio* 18 (1991): 73. Hans van den Berg has collected and published testimonies of the Aymara in *"La tierra no da asi no mas"* [The land does not give just like that] *Latin American Studies* 51 (1989).

5. From a paper by Vincent Busch, "Grounding Our Hope." Busch is a Columban priest and writer who has devoted his life to supporting indigenous peoples and combating ecological destruction in the Philippines.

6. C. Dean Freudenberger, "Caring for the Earth," *Together* (January-March 1989): 7. *Together* is the newsletter of World Vision.

7. Russell Means, taken from an address delivered by Russell Means at the 1980 Black Hills Alliance Survival Gathering, as quoted in Busch, "Grounding Our Hope."

8. Michael J. Caduto and Joseph Bruchac, *Keepers of the Earth: Native American Stories and Environmental Activities for Children* (Golden, CO: Fulcrum, Inc., 1988), p. 193.

9. "Message from the Heart of the World," *ILEIA Newsletter* (May 1991): 36.

10. "Voice of the Earth Crying To Be Heard," *Panchar Penemu* 22 (May 1992): 8.

11. Stephan Rist, "Revitalizing Indigenous Knowledge," *ILEIA Newsletter* 3/91 (October 1991): 22.

12. Dr. Ghillean Prance, "Faith and Respect for Nature," paper presented at CODEL Workshop "Care for the Earth: A Challenge to All Christians," December 1987.

13. Helena Norberg-Hodge, "Ladakh: Developing Greed in a Contented Land," *The New Road* (February-March 1992): 1ff.

14. Julian Pitchford, "In Tune with God and His Environment," *Together* (January-March 1989): 11.

15. Prayers courtesy of Vincent Busch, from an unpublished paper "A Celebrated Friendship with the Earth."

CHAPTER 4: WHAT WENT WRONG? THE ENLIGHTENMENT AND THE RISE OF INDUSTRIALIZATION

1. The authors are indebted to Drs. Mary Evelyn Tucker and Bill Gibson for insights into the Enlightenment period. Mary Evelyn Tucker authored *Moral and Spiritual Cultivation in Japanese in Neo-Confucianism: The Life and Thought of Kaibara Ekken 1630-1714* (Albany: SUNY Press, 1989). Bill Gibson is principal author for *Keeping and Healing the Creation* (1989) and *Restoring Creation for Ecology and Justice* (1990), both prepared by the Presbyterian Eco-Justice Task Force.

2. Scholars who have examined this period for its relevance to the human attitude toward nature include Mary E. Clark, *Ariadne's Thread: The Search for New Modes of Thinking* (New York: St. Martin's Press, 1989), and Carolyn Merchant, *The Death of Nature* (San Francisco: Harper, 1990).

3. Tu Wei-Ming, "Beyond the Enlightenment Mentality: An Exploration of Spiritual Resources in the Global Community," paper presented at Fourth Conference on World Spirituality, Honolulu, June 1992, p. 5.

4. Clark, *Ariadne's Thread*, p. 261.

5. Ibid. p. 269.

6. Tu Wei-Ming, "Beyond the Enlightenment Mentality," p. 6.

7. Ibid. p. 9.

8. Clark, *Ariadne's Thread*, p. 353.

9. *Brazil Primer* (Philadelphia: American Friends Service Committee, 1985).

10. Taken from *Hope for the Seeds* by Vincent Busch. By permission.

CHAPTER 6: ECOLOGICAL HEALING—A CHRISTIAN RESPONSE

1. Thomas Berry with Thomas Clarke, *Befriending the Earth: A Theology of Reconciliation Between Humans and the Earth* (Mystic, CT: Twenty-Third Publications, 1991), p. 1. Berry is also the author of *The Dream of the Earth* (San Francisco: Sierra Club, 1988) and, with Brian Swimme, of *The Universe Story* (New York: HarperCollins, 1992).

2. Brian Swimme, *The Universe Is a Green Dragon* (Santa Fe, NM: Bear & Co., 1984), p. 19.

3. Some fundamentalist Christians believe that God holds all power and has already determined the outcome of world events. In this view, humans can only make sure they individually are "right" with their Creator. They have no responsibility for the world. This happily is a minority view in Christianity. Christianity has always taught that Christians have responsibility in this world. The question is, how much?

4. Sallie McFague, *Models of God: Theology for an Ecological, Nuclear Age* (Philadelphia: Fortress Press, 1987), p. 165.

5. Ibid. p. 180.

6. Loren Wilkinson, *Earthkeeping: Christian Stewardship of Natural Resources* (Grand Rapids, MI: Wm. B. Eerdmans Publishing Company, 1980), p. 230.

7. Ibid. p. 231.

8. Aldo Leopold, *A Sand County Almanac* (New York: Oxford University Press, 1949), pp. 224-25, cited in Wilkinson, *Earthkeeping*, p. 266 and n. 4, p. 300.

9. Wilkinson, *Earthkeeping*, pp. 262-77.

10. Catholic Bishops of the Philippines, *What Is Happening to Our Beautiful Land?* (Manila, January 1988).

11. *Pastoral Letter of the Dominican Episcopal Conference* (Santo Domingo, Dominican Republic, 10 August 1982).

12. *Pastoral Letter of the Dominican Episcopal Conference* (Santo Domingo, Dominican Republic, 21 January 1987).

13. Pope John Paul II, "Peace with God the Creator, Peace with God the Creation," World Peace Day, 1 January 1990, Rome.

CHAPTER 7: ECOLOGICAL HEALING—TOWARD A SUSTAINABLE WORLD

1. Lawrence E. Sullivan, "Healing," Encyclopedia of Religion, vol. 6 (New York: Macmillan, 1987), p. 226.

2. See Mary E. Clark, *Ariadne's Thread* (New York: St. Martin's Press, 1989) p. 354.

3. Herman E. Daly, "Sustainable Growth: A Bad Oxymoron," *Orion* (Spring 1991).

4. "Women's Action Agenda 21," *World Women's Congress for a Healthy Planet: Official Report* (New York: Women's Environment & Development Organization, 1992), p. 18. Copies of the report may be obtained by sending $5 (U.S.), payable to WEDO/Women USA Fund, Inc., to World Women's Congress Report, c/o WEDO, 845 Third Avenue, 15th floor, New York, NY 10022, USA.

5. "The New World Dialogue on Environment and Development in the Western Hemisphere," *Compact for a New World* (Washington, DC: World Resources Institute, 1991), p. 23.

6. Ibid.

7. A recent study, *Sustainable Development: Changing Production Patterns, Social Equity and the Environment*, prepared by the Economic Commission for Latin America and the Caribbean (ECLAC), critically analyzes the swaps. The report may be obtained by writing the Information Service of ECLAC, Casilla 179-D, Santiago, Chile. There is also a discussion of the pros and cons of debt-for-nature swaps in the July-August 1989 issue of *Development Forum*, published by the United Nations Department of Public Information for the Joint United Nations Information Committee, PO Box 5850, Grand Central Station, New York, NY 10163-5850, USA.

8. Herman E. Daly and John B. Cobb, Jr., *For the Common Good* (Boston: Beacon, 1989).

9. North American Coalition on Religion and Ecology, *Ecoletter* (Spring 1991).

10. P. Jacobs and D. A. Munro, eds., *Conservation with Equity: Strategies for Sustainable Development*. Proceedings of the Conference on Conservation and Development: Implementing the World Conservation Strategy, Ottawa, Canada, 1986 (Gland, Switzerland: International Union for Conservation of Nature and Natural Resources, 1987), p. 20.

11. Paul Harrison, *The Greening of Africa* (London: Paladin Grafton Books, 1987). This book is a superb and useable work on which to base environmentally sound development work in Africa.

12. Miguel Altieri, *Environmentally Sound Small-Scale Agricultural Projects* (New York: CODEL, 1988).

13. Lester Brown, *State of the World 1991* (Washington, DC: Worldwatch Institute, 1991), p. 26.

14. Harrison, *The Greening of Africa*, p. 209.

15. For further information, see CODEL-VITA Guidelines for Planning Series - *Energy*.

16. *State of the World 1992*, p. 6. The recommendations in this section are based heavily on those in this report.

17. Ibid. p. 41.

18. *Official Report: World Women's Congress for a Healthy Planet*, 12 November 1991, Miami, Florida (New York: Women's Environment & Development Organization, 1992), p. 18. The report may be obtained by sending $5 (U.S.), payable to WEDO/Women USA Fund, Inc., to World Women's Congress Report, c/o WEDO, 845 Third Avenue, 15th floor, New York, NY 10022, USA. Bulk rates available on request.

19. Alan B. Durning, *Poverty and the Environment: Reversing the Downward Spiral* (Washington, DC: Worldwatch, 1989), p. 60.

20. Harrison, *The Greening of Africa*, p. 249.

21. Ibid. pp. 251-52.

22. Durning, *Poverty and the Environment*, p. 56.

23. Harrison, *The Greening of Africa*, pp. 302-5.

24. Robert Chambers, "Putting the Last First," *The Living Economy: A New Economics in the Making* (New York: Routledge & Kegan Paul, Inc., 1986). See Table 13:1.

25. Ibid. p. 319.

26. Durning, *Poverty and the Environment*, p. 57.

27. Ibid. p. 58.

28. Wendell Berry, "Out of Your Car, Off Your Horse," *The Atlantic* (February 1991), pp. 62-63.

CODEL Member Organizations

African Methodist Episcopal Church
ALM Inernational
Catholic Relief Services
Christian Brothers' Conference
Christian Children's Fund
Church of the Brethren
Church World Service & Witness
Congregation of the Holy Ghost
Divine Word Missionaries
Episcopal Church—Presiding Bishop's Fund for World Relief
Franciscan Friars
Franciscan Missionary Union
Freedom from Hunger Foundation
Greek Orthodox Archdiocese of North and South America
Heifer Project International
Lutheran World Relief
MAP International
Marist Missions
Maryknoll Fathers and Brothers
Maryknoll Sisters
Medical Mission Sisters
Mennonite Central Committee
Mill Hill Missionaries
John Milton Society for the Blind
Missionaries of Africa
Pallottines of the Immaculate Conception Province
Pax World Service
P.I.M.E. Missionaries
Society of African Missions
Society of the Holy Child Jesus
St. Columban Foreign Mission Society
Technoserve
Unitarian Universalist Service Committee
United Church Board for World Ministries
United Methodist Committee on Relief, General Board of Global
Ministries
World Vision Relief and Development, Inc.
YMCA—International Division
YWCA—National Board

The Guidelines for Planning Series on Environmentally Sound Small-Scale Projects

Environmentally Sound Small-Scale Agricultural Projects: English, French, Spanish

Environmentally Sound Small-Scale Water Projects: English, Spanish

Environmentally Sound Small-Scale Forestry Projects: English, French, Spanish

Environmentally Sound Small-Scale Energy Projects: English

Environmentally Sound Small-Scale Livestock Projects: English, Spanish

For a complete listing of these and other publications, write to:

Coordination in Development, Inc. (CODEL)
475 Riverside Drive, Room 1842
New York, N.Y. 10115 USA